IMAGES
of America

BUCKS COUNTY
TROLLEYS

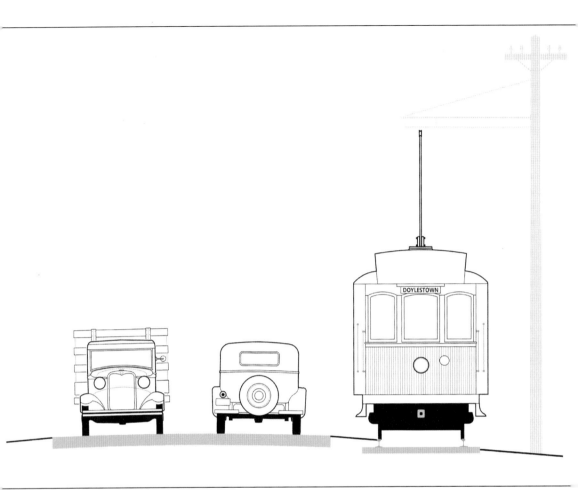

Bucks County's trolley tracks often ran alongside public roads, as depicted in this scaled drawing based on 1920s Pennsylvania Department of Highways standards. While representative of many locations throughout the county, this drawing shows Old Easton Road in Plumstead Township with a Doylestown & Easton Street Railway trolley car. The trolleys ran in both directions on the same track, with opposing trolleys passing at sidings along the line. (Drafted by the author.)

ON THE COVER: It is spring 1905, and this New Jersey and Pennsylvania Traction Company two-man crew has paused for the camera with brand-new trolley car No. 2. One of four trolleys procured to provide service on the Trenton–to–New Hope and Lambertville line, which was then under construction, the electric streetcar stands at the end of track on Washington Street at State Street in Newtown, Pennsylvania. A staircase leading up to the porch of the colonial-era Brick Hotel may be glimpsed to the right. In 1912, the rails would be extended around the corner and connected with the trolley track on State Street. The last day for Newtown trolleys would be September 20, 1924. (Courtesy of the Newtown Historic Association.)

IMAGES
of America

BUCKS COUNTY
TROLLEYS

Mike Szilagyi

ARCADIA
PUBLISHING

Copyright © 2020 by Mike Szilagyi
ISBN 978-1-4671-0520-0

Published by Arcadia Publishing
Charleston, South Carolina

Printed in the United States of America

Library of Congress Control Number: 2020930229

For all general information, please contact Arcadia Publishing:
Telephone 843-853-2070
Fax 843-853-0044
E-mail sales@arcadiapublishing.com
For customer service and orders:
Toll-Free 1-888-313-2665

Visit us on the Internet at www.arcadiapublishing.com

This volume is dedicated to the memory of Barker Gummere IV. Born in Trenton, New Jersey, Gummere earned his bachelor of arts in history from Princeton University and lived most of his life in Newtown, Bucks County. He researched and authored several books on the history of local trolleys, cowriting the authoritative *Trolleys of Bucks County Pennsylvania* in 1985. Gummere traveled widely to ride and photograph streetcars. This photograph captures him far from home in Adelaide, Australia, happily standing by one of 30 "Bay Trams" built by A. Pengelly & Co. in Adelaide. These 1920s streetcars closely resembled American trolleys of that era. Known as "Red Rattlers" in their later years, their long life span nearly equaled Gummere's. These trolleys were built in 1929 and were retired only in 2006. Barker Gummere's life spanned the years 1928 to 2009. (Courtesy of Mark C. Deren.)

CONTENTS

ACKNOWLEDGMENTS

A great many individuals and organizations contributed to this effort. Each is owed my thanks and gratitude. In composing these acknowledgments, I will do my best to mention them all. First thanks are due to rail transit historians Andrew W. Maginnis and Stanley F. Bowman Jr. Their unfailing support and generosity over the years inspired this project, as well as our previous title *Montgomery County Trolleys*. Thanks also go to Steven Cohen for sharing his incomparable collection of rare Bucks County postcards; Dr. Richard Allman for superb prints that he painstakingly developed from negatives; the late David F. Drinkhouse of Easton for his kindness and generosity in sharing his archives gathered over 20-plus years investigating every detail of the Doylestown-to-Easton trolley; Douglas E. Peters, longtime curator of Railways to Yesterday's Frederick E. Barber Memorial Library; Joseph Boscia; Richard S. Short; Joel Salomon; Edward Springer; the late James C. McHugh; William J. McKelvey Jr., director and chairman, Liberty Historic Railway of New Jersey; Edward Lybarger, archivist emeritus, Pennsylvania Trolley Museum; Charles Long, treasurer, East Penn Traction Club; David Callahan, Newtown Historic Association; Susan Taylor, Yardley Historical Association; Elizabeth Weaver, Friends of the Delaware Canal; Heather Davis, Sellersville Museum; Betty Davis, Washington Crossing Card Collectors Club; Jerry Chiccarine; Jack Fulton, Mark C. Deren, Historic Langhorne Association; Nancy Takach, verifier, Bucks County Recorder of Deeds; Stephanie Mason, manager, Doylestown Township; Karen Forbes, Doylestown Historical Society; Will Echevarria, curator of digital collections, Free Library of Philadelphia; Joshua Rowley, reference archivist, Duke University; Heather Ross, map specialist, Penn State University; Shirley Bonsall, Nockamixon Township Historical Commission; Steve Moyer and Dick Shearer of the Lansdale Historical Society; Eric Walerko, archive and exhibits coordinator, Margaret R. Grundy Memorial Library; Melissa Jay, Bucks County Historical Society's Mercer Museum; Chandra Scott, archivist, Pennsylvania Department of Transportation District No. 6; Robert Homolka, researcher and archivist, Historical Society of Bensalem Township; the Willis M. Rivinus collection of the Solebury Township Historical Society; and QNB Bank, Quakertown.

INTRODUCTION

One of three original counties of the Pennsylvania colony, Bucks County was founded by William Penn in 1682, the other counties being Chester and Philadelphia. Bucks County contained a vast area encompassing 1,347 square miles, its northern boundary following the ridge of Blue Mountain, 60 miles distant from Penn's estate at Pennsbury on the Delaware River. A 1752 partition carved out Northampton County, with the revised Bucks County boundary 40 miles northwest of Pennsbury. This left Bucks County with 622 square miles of gently rolling terrain, the topography gradually increasing in ruggedness to the north. The map on page 11 locates Bucks County in its regional context.

In 1810, the county seat was moved from Newtown to the more centrally located Doylestown. By that time, primarily agricultural in character, Bucks County was traversed only by rough earthen roads, many of which were simply widened Lenape Indian paths. William Penn's original plan for a grid of roads oriented parallel to County Line Road was only partially implemented.

The Delaware River along the county's eastern boundary with New Jersey was navigable by cargo vessels for just the downstream portion of its length, although rafts of timber, hewn from old-growth forests, had long been floated downriver from points well upstream.

After years of planning followed by five years of construction, the Delaware Division of the Pennsylvania Canal was completed in 1832. This state-funded project extended navigation from tidewater at Bristol to Morrisville and then north along the full length of the eastern edge of Bucks County. At Easton, five miles north of the county line, the Delaware Canal connected with the Lehigh Canal to reach upstate anthracite coalfields. Although animal powered, the manifold increase in efficiency unlocked a tremendous flow of bulk commodities, including coal, limestone, and cement going south and manufactured goods going north.

Rails first came to Bucks County in 1833, with the first segment of railroad built from Bristol (then and now the county's largest town) north to Morrisville. From there, connections could be made for points north, including Trenton and New York. Because a common choice for passengers from Philadelphia was to book passage on Delaware River steamships, rails were laid the length of Market Street in Bristol allowing for convenient transfer of people and goods between riverside wharves and trains. The following year, the Philadelphia & Trenton Railroad was extended south from Bristol, ultimately reaching Front and Berks Streets in the Kensington section of Philadelphia. In 1835, steam locomotives began replacing horses as motive power. So began the first iteration of the direct Philadelphia–to–New York steam railroad that would eventually become today's Northeast Corridor.

Completed in 1857, the North Pennsylvania Railroad served inland portions of western Bucks County. Built as a direct connection between Philadelphia and Pennsylvania's coal-producing region, the 15 miles of the North Penn that passed through the county enabled rapid growth of the boroughs of Telford, Sellersville, Perkasie, and Quakertown. Branching from Lansdale in adjacent Montgomery County, the seven miles of single-track Doylestown Branch that traversed Bucks County encouraged the growth of villages that would over time become the boroughs of Chalfont and New Britain. North Penn trains started and ended their trips at Front and Willow Streets in Northern Liberties.

The 1870s saw construction of steam railroads serving Newtown, Langhorne, Yardley, and Ivyland. New Hope was reached in 1891.

Heavy rail traffic on the Pennsylvania Railroad prompted the need for a freight bypass around Philadelphia. Opening in 1891, the Trenton cutoff diverged from the main track near Morrisville, passed north of Langhorne, and exited the county at Southampton. In 1899, a public road tunnel beneath the cutoff was the site of an infamous encounter between railroad crews and trolley workmen known as the "Battle of Langhorne" (see page 36).

The final steam railroad built in Bucks County was the Quakertown & Eastern (Q&E). Inaugurating service in 1901, Q&E's 15-mile single track connected the Reading Railroad at Quakertown with Durham Furnace on the Delaware River. Durham Furnace was one of Bucks County's earliest industrial sites, having produced its first iron in 1728. What had been a prime location for industry centuries earlier could not compete with modern facilities; the works were no longer profitable and, ironically, closed just as the railroad was completed. In 1903, the *Bucks County Gazette* informed its readers that the Q&E's slow and seemingly random service earned it the local sobriquets the "Quiet & Easy" and "Queer & Eccentric." The 1907 suspension of railroad service on the Q&E would be of great benefit to some trolley passengers; this is explained on page 107. Although plans were floated to resurrect the Q&E as an electric trolley line, this was never done.

The completion of the steam railroads left large swaths of Bucks County without rail service and still reliant on animal-powered wagons, plodding along rough, unpaved roads. The development of concrete and asphalt "permanent" paving materials was still decades in the future. Hard rain or spring snowmelt left roads literally knee deep in mud. Despite the condition of the roads, a 1913 statewide referendum seeking the electorate's consent to borrow $50 million to pave roads went down in defeat. Even as late as 1920, conditions could be brutal, as this *Bristol Daily Courier* article describing a busy stretch of road in Falls Township attests:

> This is the great Lincoln Highway . . . the main line of automobile transportation between Philadelphia and New York. Day and night a continuous stream of heavily loaded trucks and pleasure cars labor over this burlesque turnpike. And all the hours are filled with the sounds of breaking springs, the slosh of mud in three-foot holes and the cries of unstrung truck drivers. The fact is the only way one can tell the Lincoln Highway from the open fields at this point is that there is no grass on it and that it is a good bit rougher than the fields. At some places it looks like it has been heavily shelled for a couple of weeks. One deep, water-filled hole follows another. The only attempt to repair this condition has been the dumping of a few loads of crushed rocks at different points, which, though annoying to drivers, really do not make the road much worse.

Despite the chronic poor condition of the road system, the steam railroads could not build a network dense enough to serve all of the county. The simple physics of a single powerful locomotive pulling a long string of cars placed constraints on where and how railroads could be built. Steam trains required virtually level, gradually curving track geometry. Threading a steam railroad through Bucks County's varied and hilly terrain required tremendous cuts and fills, the erection of bridges, and boring of tunnels, all of which were expensive. A landscape of scattered farming communities and small towns did not warrant the investment.

The emerging technology of electric railcars—trolleys—changed all that. Electric trolleys climbed hills easily and navigated tight turns, like curves around city street corners. While steam railroads needed to procure right-of-way for their routes, trolley promoters had the option of simply laying tracks along public roads; however, there were limits to this. Stretches of railroad-style private right-of-way were also built for the trolleys where it made sense. In contrast to steam trains that may stop at only one station in a town, the electric trolley would often be routed right up a town's main street and would allow passengers on and off at each corner. Lower fares and more frequent service (often hourly or better) sealed the deal. The trolley was a huge hit.

In the 1890s, electric trolleys were all the rage across the United States. Civic-minded townsfolk felt that a trolley line would "put them on the map," and in fact cheap, convenient mass transit was a boon to commerce. Access to higher education was made possible also. In her book *Trolley Memories of a Raubsville Resident*, Jane Kiefer Leary explains that the mobility provided by the Doylestown-to-Easton trolley enabled her education to progress beyond the grade school level provided by the local elementary school.

The front page of the May 6, 1897, issue of the *Bucks County Gazette* relates the following:

Mr. Benjamin J. Taylor, President of the Farmers National Bank, is a great believer in trolleys. He says he has three farms on the line between Bristol and Langhorne, which heretofore had not been bringing him in anything, and that it was very hard to get a tenant of any kind for them. But, since the advent of the trolley, he has had a number of applicants for the rental of the farms from the very best class of farmers. He does not see why any one should oppose trolleys, and thinks that after a while a farm without a trolley line running by it will be left out in the cold just as much as a town is to-day without a water supply, or electric lights. Up to date farmers want the advantages which quick transportation to the nearest markets affords.

Steam railroads in the United States have always made good use of the right of eminent domain; that is, the right to take property without the landowner's permission. The only proviso is that the owner must be offered reasonable compensation. In Pennsylvania, trolley promoters enjoyed no such right, and railroad interests fought to keep it that way. The Young Bill, intended to extend the right of eminent domain to the trolley companies, was introduced in the state legislature in the spring of 1897. After bitterly contested debates in the state house, the Young Bill was defeated. The June 30, 1897, issue of the *Allentown Democrat* opined that "the steam railroads probably had too much boodle." The quaint term alluded to cash used to improperly buy influence.

Bucks County trolleys made their debut not in the county seat of Doylestown nor in its largest town of Bristol, but in Langhorne Borough. On April 18, 1896, a compact four-wheel electric streetcar lettered LANGHORNE connected the Reading Railroad train station with the leafy residential neighborhoods along Bellevue Avenue. Later that year, rails were extended south through Hulmeville to Bristol and, in December 1897, north to Newtown. In February 1900, trolleys from Newtown entered Doylestown on Green Street. This largely rural line, despite being equipped with modern steel trolleys in 1921, was the first to be abandoned in Bucks County, closing out service on October 31, 1923.

Begun in 1896 but not completed until 1903, the Trenton, Bristol & Philadelphia (TB&P) Street Railway connected those locations by way of Croydon, Tullytown, and Morrisville. A short gap was closed in Bristol in 1911 when the Pennsylvania Railroad built a new grade-separated line and finally allowed trolley tracks to be laid across the Mill Street grade crossing. TB&P trolleys were gradually phased out by buses between 1929 and 1932.

Between 1897 and 1901, a series of trolley lines was built that would ultimately coalesce into Lehigh Valley Transit (LVT) Company's Philadelphia Division. Built to connect Philadelphia and Allentown and upgraded in 1912 to high-speed line status, 17 miles of this line traversed western Bucks County. Towns served included Perkasie, Sellersville, and Quakertown with a (non–high speed) branch to Richlandtown. A potentially viable link from Perkasie to Doylestown was contemplated but never built.

May 24, 1898, marked the eagerly awaited introduction of Doylestown–to–Willow Grove trolleys. This 1899 notice reminds us not to idealize the past: "A reward of $200 has been offered for the arrest of wire thieves who have twice seriously crippled the line between Doylestown and Willow Grove." Freight trolleys plied the single track along Easton Road until June 1922; passenger trolleys made their last runs on February 14, 1931, Valentine's Day.

Most of the Doylestown & Easton (D&E) trolley's 32 miles were located in Bucks County. Completed in 1904, the scenic beauty of this line, advertised as the Road of Wild Roses, made it a tourist destination. While electricity for most trolleys was generated at coal-burning plants, the D&E was unique in that its trolley wire was energized with renewable hydroelectric power generated just north of the Bucks County line at Groundhog Lock on the Delaware Canal. Doylestown-to-Easton trolley service came to an end on Thanksgiving Day 1926.

1905 saw the completion of a picturesque electric trolley line north from Yardley through Washington Crossing to New Hope and Lambertville. In 1915, sufficient freight was being hauled by trolleys to warrant the construction of a track extension to a new freight station on North Main Street in New Hope. The south end of the line was an off-street terminal a short walk from the New Jersey State House in Trenton. Trolley service beyond Yardley was discontinued after September 20, 1924. Streetcars continued to run between Trenton, Morrisville, and Yardley until 1934.

In 1907, Gov. Edwin S. Stuart signed into law the McClain-Homsher Bill, granting trolley companies the right to carry freight. State grange master William T. Creasy had lobbied on behalf of farmers. However, Creasy's proposal for a proviso requiring trolley companies to haul freight was not included in the bill, as the March 26, 1907, issue of the *Harrisburg Courier* relates: "This was resisted by the greatest vehemence and some profanity . . . the Speaker came down from his handsome podium and engaged in the debate and finally Creasy was defeated." Prior to this legislation, trolleys were limited to carrying US Mail, newspapers, and small parcels. Regularly scheduled trolley freight service was essential to all manner of businesses located along the lines. A typical trolley freight station may be seen in the photograph at the top of page 18.

The last trolley track built in Bucks County was 1.5 miles of new railroad-style trolley line, completed in 1925 by Lehigh Valley Transit Company in Milford and Springfield Townships. This improvement enabled LVT to remove the side-of-the-road track along Old Bethlehem Pike in Zion Hill. The last trolley line built was also the last to be abandoned, with passenger and freight trolleys providing service until the final run of the Liberty Bell high-speed line on September 6, 1951.

This brief introduction to the early history of transportation in Bucks County is intended as a summary rather than a detailed history. Two excellent books, published in 1966 and 1985 respectively, tell the full story of Bucks County's trolleys. Interested readers are urged to seek out copies of *Trenton-Princeton Traction Company: Pennsylvania and New Jersey Railway* by Barker Gummere and Gary Kleinedler, and *Trolleys of Bucks County Pennsylvania* by Harry Foesig, Barker Gummere, and Harold E. Cox. Both books describe the planning and building of Bucks County's trolley lines, their convoluted corporate histories and mergers, and finally, the trolleys' slow decline and abandonment. In a way, the book you hold in your hands may be thought of as an illustrated companion to those authoritative volumes.

By the 1920s, the construction of a taxpayer-funded road network undercut the viability of the privately owned trolley companies. Mass transit was expected to cover its costs entirely with farebox revenue, with no public support whatsoever. The shortsighted policy of devoting public funds to subsidize motor vehicle infrastructure only—and public transit not at all—led to a financial situation that deteriorated with each passing year. Bucks County's trolleys held on as best they could, but with the single exception of the Liberty Bell high-speed line, most were forced out of business in the decade between 1923 and 1934. In response to a 1925 rumor that the Doylestown-to-Easton trolley might be abandoned, the *Bristol Daily Courier* had this to say:

> If the Easton trolley line is scrapped it will mark the passing of one of the greatest monuments to the optimism of a few men that Bucks County has ever had. Facing what seemed to be insurmountable handicaps, and in the face of pessimism which would have discouraged less optimistic souls, a few middle Bucks County men . . . risked practically their financial all on the success of the road—and built its 32 miles of line despite all of the financial and engineering difficulties presented.

The newspaper singled out the efforts of Plumsteadville entrepreneur Aaron Kratz for recognition:

> One of these men, the late Aaron Kratz whose work did a great deal toward making it [the Doylestown to Easton trolley] possible, said a few years ago that he sunk almost his whole fortune, accumulated in a life-time of successful carriage manufacturing, in the project— and had no regrets. In 1921, Mr. Kratz stated he had put $100,000 in the road [$3 million in 2020 dollars] and said publicly that "I believe I have done my duty to Bucks County."

Indeed, he did. This book represents a sincere effort to ensure that the memory of Bucks County's trolleys lives on.

One

BUCKS COUNTY TROLLEY MAPS

AN OVERVIEW

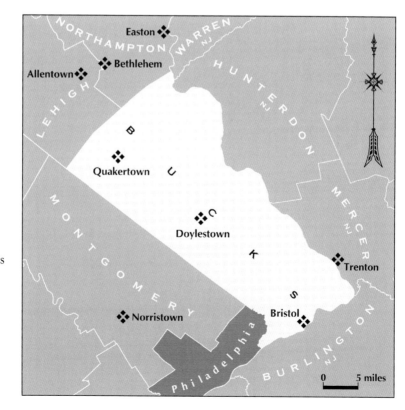

This map highlights Bucks County with surrounding counties. The overall trolley map of Bucks County may be viewed on the following two pages. (Drafted by the author.)

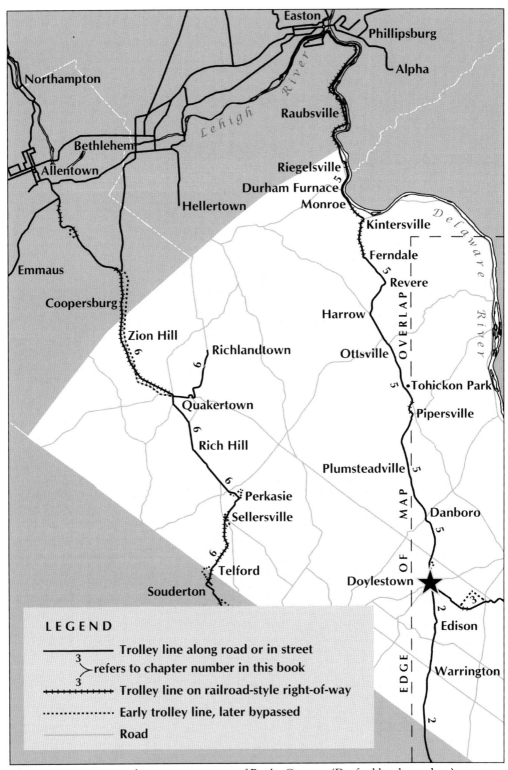

This map encompasses the western portion of Bucks County. (Drafted by the author.)

TROLLEY LINES
IN AND AROUND
BUCKS COUNTY
PENNSYLVANIA

Delaware

OVERLAP

MAP

OF

EDGE

Danboro

Doylestown

Edison

Warrington

Hatboro

Willow Grove

Frankford

Wycombe

Brownsburg

Washington
Crossing

Stoopville

Wrightstown

Newtown

Hulmeville

Croydon

Cornwells

Riverside

New Hope

Lambertville

Yardley

Langhorne

Tullytown

Bristol

Burlington

Hopewell

Pennington

Trenton
Jct.

Trenton

Morrisville

Roebling

River

Philadelphia

0   5 miles

This map encompasses the eastern portion of Bucks County. (Drafted by the author.)

13

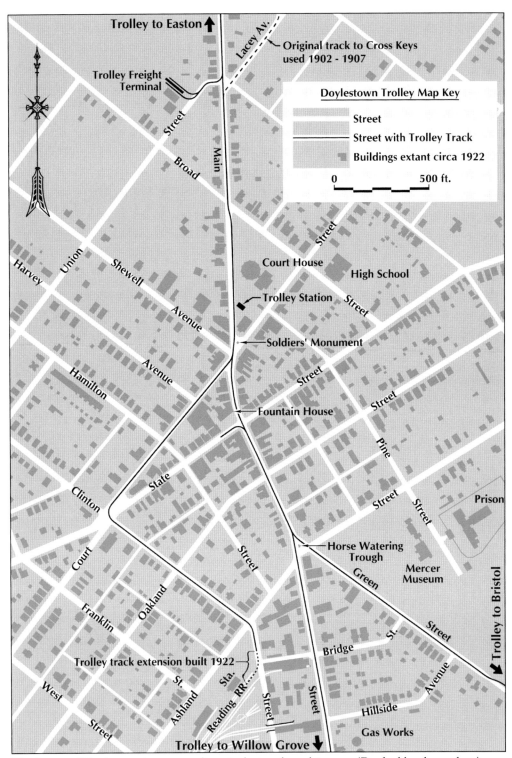

The layout of Doylestown's streetcar lines is depicted on this map. (Drafted by the author.)

Two

DOYLESTOWN, EDISON, WARRINGTON

TROLLEYS TO WILLOW GROVE

The Bucks County Railway Company offered free trolley rides from Doylestown to the historic Old Turk's Head tavern a mile south of town on opening day, May 24, 1898. With its single track on the shoulder of Easton Road, the far end of the line was 12 miles south at Willow Grove. Philadelphia's Union Traction (later Philadelphia Rapid Transit) bought the trolley line and provided service with electric streetcars until gasoline-burning buses took over in February 1931. (Courtesy of James C. McHugh.)

During the first years of service, the Doylestown–to–Willow Grove trolley track curved off Main Street, with the end of track on State Street in front of Doylestown's Fountain House tavern. Later, the track on State Street was removed, and trolleys continued up Main Street to the block above Monument Square. It is hoped that the bicycle propped against the side of this red-and-white trolley was moved before the next departure. (Courtesy of James C. McHugh.)

It is midday on Thursday, March 11, 1909, and traffic on South Main Street in Doylestown consists of precisely two horse-drawn wagons. Willow Grove trolleys entered town on this track. Barely visible on Green Street is the trolley track to Newtown and Bristol. In 1910, a track switch would join the two lines here. The corner of a horse watering trough is visible on the right. (Courtesy of the Free Library of Philadelphia, Print and Picture Department.)

North Main Street extends to the left and State Street to the right in this c. 1900 view of Monument Square. Doylestown National Bank and the 1868 Civil War Monument preside over the intersection. Here, the trolley track transitions from the center of Main Street to the east curb lane. A first-floor window of the white plaster trolley terminal can be seen between the trolley and the bank. (Courtesy of Steven Cohen.)

The photographer has set his tripod on Easton Road just below the Doylestown Borough line on March 11, 1909. The spire to the left is the clock tower of the old Bucks County Courthouse. When rails were laid in 1898, the trolley line simply followed the roadside over hill and dale. The sign on the shed at right reads, "Rifle Range." In 1973, the Route 202 bypass interchange was built here. (Courtesy of the Free Library of Philadelphia, Print and Picture Department.)

Freight was an important aspect of trolley service. In September 1909, Philadelphia Rapid Transit (PRT) Company constructed trackside freight stations at Neshaminy, Warrington, and Edison and a trolley freight terminal on Union Street in Doylestown. In Philadelphia, most trolley freight trips began and ended at PRT's trolley freight terminal at Front and Market Streets in the riverfront warehouse district. The view above looks north on Easton Road at Street Road in Warrington Township. The porch of the tollhouse is just visible behind the Neshaminy freight station. Delivery of goods from the freight station to outlying destinations was by horse-drawn wagon. The view below looks south at the same location. Worthington's general store, which housed the Neshaminy Post Office, is on the right. Today, Easton Road is five lanes wide at this location, and the roadside has been obliterated. (Both, courtesy of the Pennsylvania Trolley Museum.)

PRT No. 2607, the first Doylestown milk car, pulls into the North Philadelphia trolley freight terminal on Huntingdon Street at Sixteenth Street. Painted orange and yellow, and with boards installed inside to protect plateglass windows from shifting cargo, this trolley was rebuilt from an obsolete Philadelphia cable car. Dependable daily delivery of milk to creameries was essential to dairy farmers along the trolley line. (Courtesy of the Free Library of Philadelphia, Print and Picture Department.)

In 1913, PRT took delivery of a refrigerated freight motor. In contrast to most freight trolleys' origins as repurposed old passenger cars, F-22 was built new by J.G. Brill Company and assigned to the Doylestown line. Later renumbered T-16, this trolley served for decades as a trash collection car on the Market Frankford Subway Elevated. In 1982, it was purchased by the Pennsylvania Trolley Museum in Washington, Pennsylvania, and is today stored indoors awaiting restoration. (Courtesy of the Free Library of Philadelphia, Print and Picture Department.)

Time has not been kind to the village of Edison in Doylestown Township. Nothing remains of this scene looking north on Easton Road at the intersection with Turk Road. The catenary overhead wire system installed in 1909 is clearly visible, as well as the concrete roadway paved in 1920. Installing a second track between Doylestown and Willow Grove was proposed but never done. (Photograph by Milton Rutherford, courtesy of Doylestown Township.)

Leedom's typifies the roadside refreshment stands that lined state highways in the 1920s. The location is the village of Edison, along Easton Road north of Turk Road. PRT's Doylestown–to–Willow Grove roadside trolley track is in the foreground. The two-lane concrete highway is between the tracks and the store. Grape arbors, such as the one behind the store, were a fixture in many backyards around this time. (Courtesy of the Russell Loux collection, Doylestown Township.)

The Old Turk's Head tavern, on the east side of Easton Road just north of the village of Edison, could be reached by trolley. A century earlier, in 1808, proprietor Septimus Hough had lobbied to have the county seat moved from Newtown to this location, rather than Doylestown. The Old Turk's Head served as a Doylestown Township polling place until it was razed in 1916. (Courtesy of the collection of the Mercer Museum, Bucks County Historical Society.)

This view captures a wood-frame gasoline station being built on the east side of Easton Road, south of the intersection with Turk Road in Edison. The north-facing view also includes a glimpse of the Crystal Dance Palace on the right. The bicycle tire tracks pressed into the mud in the foreground are a reminder that bicyclists were navigating the narrow strip hemmed in between the concrete highway and the trolley track. (Courtesy of the Russell Loux collection, Doylestown Township.)

This seven-arch stone bridge carried Easton Road over Neshaminy Creek just south of the village of Edison. This location was also referred to as Bridgepoint. This north-facing photograph captures a Willow Grove–bound open trolley car on the bridge. To the left of the trolley in the distance stands the old creek-side building that housed the school of landscape painters known as the Scumblers. (Courtesy of Stanley F. Bowman Jr.)

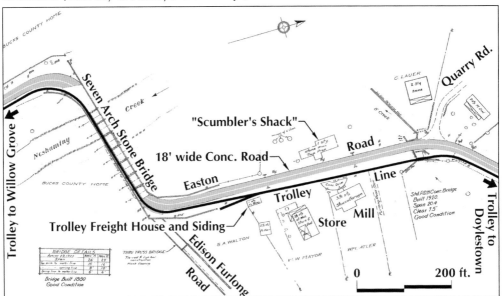

This map provides details of the village labeled on maps variously as Bridgepoint and Edison. The thick line delineates the single trolley track that followed the east side of Easton Road. The siding at the trolley freight station allowed a freight trolley to be stored there without blocking the through track. This map is based on a 1927 Pennsylvania Department of Highways right-of-way plan on file at the Bucks County Recorder of Deeds. (Drafted by the author.)

This December 1909 view looks north on Easton Road in Bridgepoint in Doylestown Township, including the trolley freight station with the trackside loading platform just beyond. Both the three-story mill and the stone house still stand today. This is one of hundreds of PRT photographs donated to the Free Library of Philadelphia in the 1940s by John Gibb Smith (see page 119). (Courtesy of the Free Library of Philadelphia, Print and Picture Department.)

The historic stone bridge over Neshaminy Creek was demolished years ago, but the highway approach on the east side of the creek is still in place. Embedded in the 1920 cement roadway, and still to be seen today, are the curving rails of the Doylestown–to–Willow Grove trolley line, which, after 1913, was referred to as PRT Route 22. The location is the intersection of Edison Road and Edison Furlong Road. (Photograph by the author.)

This September 29, 1908, photograph looks north on Easton Road from a point one mile north of Street Road in rural Warrington Township. The simple overhead trolley wire has not yet been replaced with catenary. Today, Warrington Fire Company No. 1 occupies the space on the west side of the highway where the white barns once stood. (Courtesy of the Free Library of Philadelphia, Print and Picture Department.)

This photograph from the George M. Hart collection bears the inscription "Newville Toboggan." Newville was the old name for the crossroads of Easton and Bristol Roads. Before extensive reconstruction of the line took place in 1902, the track had deteriorated, giving the trolleys an uneven ride. The speed attained by the early trolley cars, assisted by gravity on the long downhill north of the village, doubtless inspired the nickname. (Courtesy of the collection of the Mercer Museum, Bucks County Historical Society.)

Above, the crew of PRT electrical test car No. 689 pauses for a photograph on the passing siding on Easton Road north of Bristol Road in Warrington Township on August 20, 1909. This car was built in the 1880s as a Philadelphia Traction Company cable car. It was rebuilt as an electric trolley in Haverford Shops in 1894. In 1906, the car was fitted with sophisticated test gear (below) to precisely measure voltage and verify the integrity of the overhead power distribution system. In 1909, PRT replaced the Doylestown to Willow Grove line's simple overhead trolley wire with a state-of-the-art catenary wire system. It is not clear why PRT went to the expense. Foesig and Gummere point out that catenary was "an unusual innovation for a single-track country line using single-truck cars." (Both, courtesy of the Free Library of Philadelphia, Print and Picture Department.)

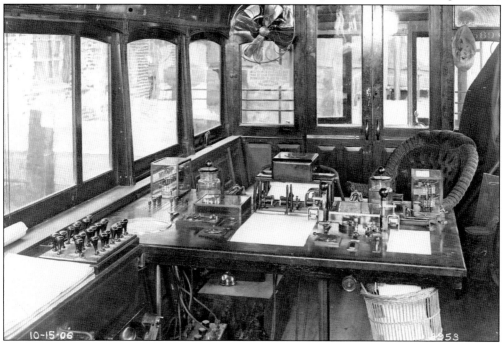

Located at the midway point between Doylestown and Willow Grove, the locale known as Frog Hollow was chosen for the trolley line's 1897 carbarn and power-generating station. This south-facing postcard view captures the narrow stone arch bridge that carried Easton Road over Little Neshaminy Creek, with the Paul Valley powerhouse, carbarn, and a trolley beyond. Cattle graze in the creek-side meadow. This postcard was published by Arnold Brothers of Rushland, Pennsylvania, as card No. 60 of their Bucks County Views series. Included on the card is the following information: "Inscription on bridge: Bucks County Bridge, 1821, 20 m to P." (Courtesy of Stanley F. Bowman Jr.)

The Paul Valley power plant was sited at a location that offered abundant water, but no canal nor railroad for the delivery of coal. Both coal and water are essential for the generation of electric power by steam. Car No. 2668's sole purpose was to shuttle carloads of coal five miles from the Pennsylvania Railroad's Trenton cutoff in Upper Moreland. (Courtesy of the Free Library of Philadelphia, Print and Picture Department.)

Bucks County Railway Company's Paul Valley facilities housed its fleet of trolley cars and generated the electricity required to run them. The initial seven cars were soon joined by more, as traffic to Willow Grove Park surged. The 50-foot-wide-by-110-foot-deep barn provided adequate capacity. Documents record that "equipment of the power house comprises two Sterling boilers, of 200 horse power each . . . two McEwen engines, of 200 horse power each [and] two Thompson & Ryan dynamos of 150 kilowatts each." A stable attached to the south end of the complex housed horses and an emergency wagon poised to respond to incidents along the line when the wires were deenergized. The powerhouse building still stands today at 429 Easton Road, Warrington. (Above, courtesy of the Pennsylvania Trolley Museum; below, courtesy of the Free Library of Philadelphia, Print and Picture Department.)

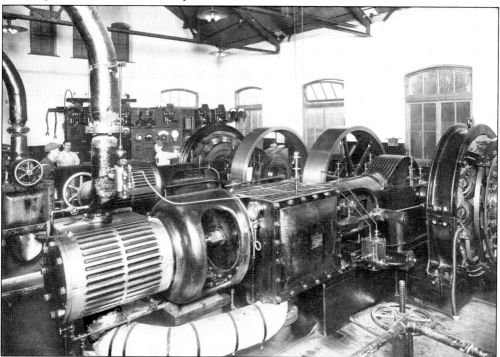

The final trolleys assigned to the line prior to its 1931 demise were relatively modern steel cars of the sort used on city streets in Philadelphia. In 1926, eight of these, operated out of Willow Grove carbarn, had been modified to be run by one man without a conductor. On these trolleys, the motorman had the option of opening doors on either side of the car, so that passengers could step off the trolley away from motor vehicle traffic. PRT double-end cars were painted orange and cream, with dark red doors. (Illustration by the author.)

Beginning in 1927, PRT offered express bus service from Broad and Locust Streets in Philadelphia through Doylestown to Easton. At first, local service between Doylestown and Willow Grove was still provided by streetcars. But after February 14, 1931, all service was provided by gasoline-powered buses, and the electric trolley line was abandoned. Philadelphia Rural Transit Company was PRT's bus subsidiary. These sketches were featured on PRT brochures and bus schedules. (Left, courtesy of Joseph Boscia; right, courtesy of Edward Springer.)

Three

YARDLEY, NEWTOWN, NEW HOPE

BUCKS COUNTY ELECTRIC RAILWAY

Bucks County Electric Railway, known in later years as the Pennsylvania–New Jersey (PA-NJ) Railway, was the largest trolley system in Bucks County, with 48 route miles. After crossing the Calhoun Street Bridge over the Delaware River, trolley lines branched out to serve Morrisville, Yardley, Newtown, New Hope, and Lambertville. Another line joined Bristol and Doylestown through Hulmeville, Langhorne, and Newtown. This view captures a patriotic parade in New Hope passing a Trenton-bound trolley. The stone building is the Parry Mansion, today home of the New Hope Historical Society. (Courtesy of the Steven D. Maguire collection, James C. McHugh.)

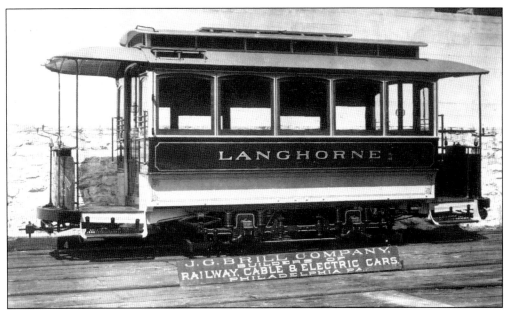

Bucks County's first electric trolley car carried its first passengers on April 18, 1896. That summer, between 300 and 400 passengers a day rode the 1.75-mile line connecting the Langhorne train station with the northern borough limits. Thirty-five round trips per day were scheduled. Soon, the line was extended south to Bristol and north to Newtown, and steadily increasing ridership meant larger trolley cars were added to the roster. (Courtesy of Andrew W. Maginnis.)

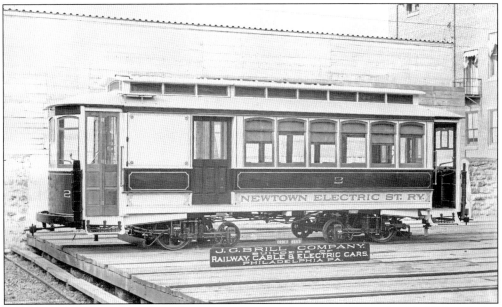

Newtown Electric Street Railway Company inaugurated service on December 21, 1897, with this combination baggage-and-passenger trolley. Because the Pennsylvania Railroad refused to allow trolley tracks to be laid through the public road tunnel beneath the railroad north of Langhorne, passengers were forced to disembark and walk through the tunnel to continue on board another trolley. This unfortunate situation came to a head two years later (see page 36). (Courtesy of the Pennsylvania Trolley Museum.)

This c. 1912 photograph captures a helpful conductor assisting a passenger climbing aboard car No. 16 in Langhorne. The view is looking south on Bellevue Avenue at Richardson Avenue. In the first years of the line, a small carbarn had housed trolleys at the corner of Bellevue and Watson Avenues. Car No. 16 was a single-truck closed car purchased secondhand from Philadelphia Rapid Transit Company. (Courtesy of James C. McHugh.)

Doylestown-to-Bristol service started on February 25, 1900. This c. 1905 view finds car No. 3 nearing the village of Stoopville, 11 miles into its 26-mile run from Doylestown. The faded lettering on the side of the car was short for Newtown, Langhorne & Bristol Trolley Street Railway Company. The vintage 1896 trolley would soon be scrapped, but the house still stands at 124 Stoopville Road in Newtown Township. (Courtesy of Newtown Historic Association.)

The crew of car No. 5 awaits departure for Trenton, New Jersey, from the corner of Washington Avenue and State Street in Newtown. The porch of the historic Brick Hotel may be glimpsed on the left. Rails of the Doylestown-to-Bristol trolley line cross in the foreground. Car No. 5 is at the same location as the trolley on the front cover of this book but viewed from the opposite vantage point. (Courtesy of Steven Cohen.)

An open trolley car rolls away from the camera eastbound on Bridge Street from the corner of Pennsylvania Avenue (then called Smith Street) in Morrisville. Beginning on May 8, 1901, trolleys ran in the following counter-clockwise direction through the borough: west on Trenton Avenue, south on Pennsylvania Avenue, east on Bridge Street, and north on Delmorr Avenue (then called Mill Street). Trolleys used the Calhoun Street Bridge over the Delaware River to access Trenton. (Courtesy of Steven Cohen.)

Trolleys from Doylestown ended their runs here on Bath Street at Otter Street in Bristol. The rails simply ended in the middle of the street, with no track connection with the Trenton-to-Philadelphia trolley track on Otter Street. In September 1916, a runaway trolley gathered up another trolley, the impromptu "train" running two miles into town before splintering a utility pole on the far side of Otter Street. The Trenton to Philadelphia line was held up until the smashed trolleys could be removed. (Courtesy of the Margaret R. Grundy Memorial Library.)

This view of double-truck open car No. 6 looks south on Bath Street in Bristol, illustrating a common problem that arose when trolley lines were built. Often, unpaved streets did not conform to the proposed street grade, but the new trolley tracks did. Here, the rails are considerably higher than the rest of the street. The first two houses on the left were demolished when the Pennsylvania Railroad completed its Bristol grade-separation project in 1911. (Courtesy of the Pennsylvania Trolley Museum.)

Aside from the handwritten notation, "Langhorne Eden 1908 to 1913," not much is known about the location of this photograph. The roadside track is typical of Bucks County's trolley lines, which were built along the edges of dirt roads between towns. The building at left with the architectural scroll at the roofline is distinctive. Car No. 12 was an 1899 product of the St. Louis Car Company. (Courtesy of James C. McHugh.)

From the beginning of trolley service in 1896 to the end in 1923, Doylestown-to-Bristol trolleys offered convenient transfer to and from Reading Railroad passenger trains at Langhorne Station. The overhead sign in this view indicates hourly trolley service, with half hourly weekend service during summer months. Once the photographer has his photograph, car No. 12 will leave for Bristol. (Courtesy of Newtown Historic Association.)

In 1908, the trolley system headquartered in Newtown was known as the Bucks County Electric Railway Company. The year 1913 saw the corporate name changed to Bucks County Interurban Railway Company and, finally, the New Jersey & Pennsylvania Railway Company in 1917. Car No. 14 is headed away from the camera north on Bath Street in Bristol during the Pennsylvania Railroad's grade-separation project, completed in 1911. (Courtesy of Andrew W. Maginnis.)

In 1907, this primitive bus carried passengers between Langhorne and Morrisville. Often, lack of capital meant that proposed trolley lines were never built, and in some cases, bus service was tried. The passengers' only protection from the elements was canvas side curtains that could be rolled down. The notorious conditions of rutted earth-surface roads made for a rough ride. (Courtesy of the Pennsylvania Trolley Museum.)

The established steam railroads tried to block the construction of trolley lines whenever possible. Crews hired by competing interests attacked one another's work and each other. The "Battle of Langhorne" occurred on May 12, 1899. The Pennsylvania Railroad's ethnic German and Irish workmen lowered a hook from above the road tunnel north of Langhorne, ripping up the trolley rails and tipping this trolley over on its side (above). The trolley builders were Italian immigrants; Foesig and Gummere wryly noted that "the fight was enlivened by cursing in three languages." When a Newtown fire engine aimed high-pressure water at the railroad men, they responded by piercing the fire hose with pickaxes. After months of litigation, an agreement was reached, and through trolley service commenced on October 21, 1899. The trolley track branching to the right below enabled a work trolley to bring coal from the railroad to the power plant at Newtown. (Above, courtesy of the Newtown Historic Association; below, photograph by W. Justin Stradling, courtesy of the Pennsylvania Trolley Museum.)

The three-story building that housed Henry's Store and Neshaminy Lodge No. 422, International Order of Odd Fellows, still stands at Hulme and Main Streets in Hulmeville. Earth piled on the rails indicates work is being done on the trolley line. The bicycles leaning against the porch are a reminder that cycling was quite popular in the years before the prevalence of the automobile made sharing the roads less pleasant and decidedly less safe. (Courtesy of Steven Cohen.)

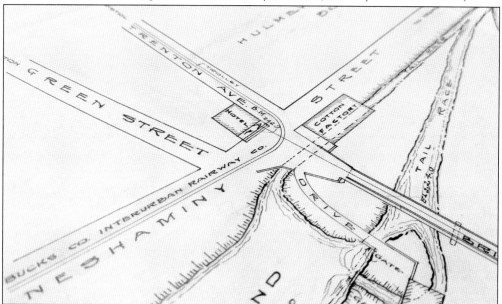

This 1917 drawing was prepared in the office of Doylestown architect and engineer A. Oscar Martin in preparation for the replacement of the old steel Hulmeville bridge over Neshaminy Creek. Clearly visible is the trolley track, labeled Bucks County Interurban Railway Company, including the tight curve between the hotel and a cotton factory. The precision of the ink-on-linen (also known as Columbia cloth) drafting is superb. (Courtesy of the collection of the Mercer Museum, Bucks County Historical Society.)

The largest structure on the Bristol-to-Doylestown line was the trolley trestle at Wycombe. Built in 1899 and extensively rebuilt in 1912, multiple spans crossed Mill Creek, the New Hope Branch of the Reading Railroad, and Mill Creek Road. This May 14, 1907, view looks south with a Doylestown-bound trolley car hurrying over the steel pony truss bridge. This Arnold Brothers photograph was published as postcard No. 64 of the Bucks County Views series. (Courtesy of the Pennsylvania Trolley Museum.)

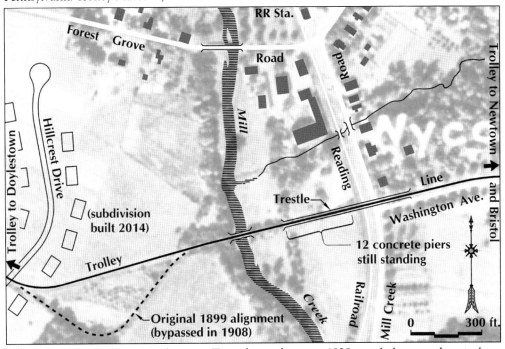

This map of Wycombe in Wrightstown Township utilizes a c. 1928 aerial photograph as its base layer. The trolley line had been abandoned about five years prior. The original and revised trolley track alignments are highlighted, as are significant topographic and man-made features. (Drafted by the author.)

This photograph captures the length of the original 1899 Wycombe trestle, most of which was built of heavy wood timbers. The double width of the steel truss span provided space for a second track, an indication of just how confident the builders were in the future success of the line. Enough trolley traffic to warrant a second track never materialized. (Courtesy of Newtown Historic Association.)

This track on Green Street was used by Bristol and Newtown trolleys as they entered the borough of Doylestown. The photograph for this postcard view must have been taken prior to 1904. Construction had not yet started on Bucks County Historical Society's Elkins Building, nor on Henry Mercer's six-story concrete museum, both of which would occupy the field on the right side of the road. (Courtesy of Steven Cohen.)

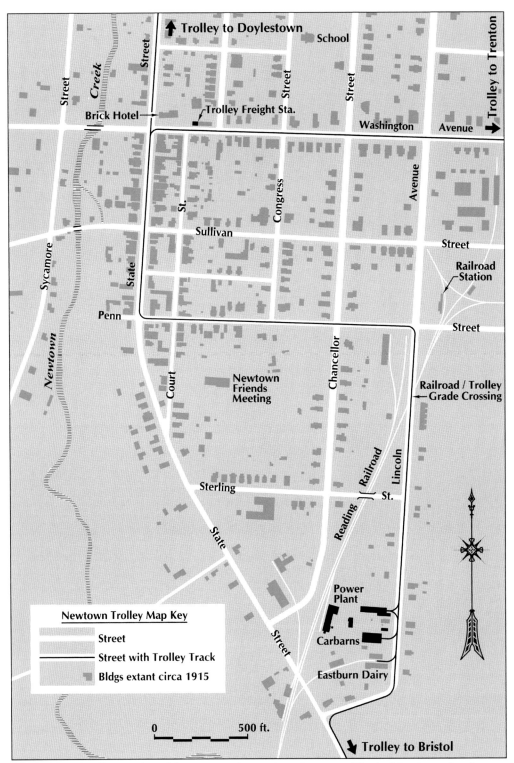

The layout of trolley tracks in Newtown is depicted on this map. (Drafted by the author.)

Car No. 11, built by Philadelphia's J.G. Brill Company in 1911, stands in the center of North State Street at Jefferson Street in Newtown. The role of the mustachioed man standing in the vestibule is not known, but he is not dressed as a motorman nor as a conductor. The substantial stone houses behind the trolley still stand at 159 (left) and 155 (right) North State Street. (Courtesy of the Newtown Historic Association.)

Bucks County Electric Railway car No. 7 loads passengers on Washington Avenue at State Street in Newtown. The trolley has been chartered this day to carry the Newtown basketball team to a league game in Lawrenceville, New Jersey. Car No. 7 would go on to serve a remarkable total of 37 years, still in working order when the Yardley and Morrisville lines were shut down in 1934. (Courtesy of James C. McHugh.)

Employees of the Bucks County Electric Railway stand on the steps of the company office on South Lincoln Avenue in Newtown. Trolley carbarns stood initially on the right side and, later, on both sides of the office building. The men are identified as, from left to right, Anselm Bohmler, Jake Gumpper, Joe Webster, and Joseph Gumpper. In 1914, Joseph Gumpper was appointed superintendent of the Bristol–Doylestown division of the trolley line. (Courtesy of the Newtown Historic Association.)

No fleet number is visible, but this trolley is likely car No. 9, the same trolley that inaugurated Bucks County trolley service in 1896 with LANGHORNE lettered on its sides. With its 16-foot-long body limiting its capacity, it has been pressed into service as a work car, here towing trailers loaded with a wooden line pole. The location is South Lincoln Avenue in Newtown. The round clock embedded in the wall above the door of the trolley office building can be seen to the right. (Courtesy of the Newtown Historic Association.)

This 1913 view of the Eastburn dairy in Newtown captures milk cans being unloaded from a Bucks County Electric Railway freight trolley. Dependable daily delivery of milk to dairies and creameries, as well as the return of the empty cans each day, was of great convenience to farmers. The driver of the Packard is identified as William B. Fabian, and the passenger is a Mr. Blackfin. These buildings still stand at 358 South Lincoln Avenue, Newtown. (Courtesy of the Newtown Historic Association.)

This rare 1920s photograph captures a Doylestown-bound trolley car along Eagle Road in Newtown Township. The view looks south from the location where Blayze Court is today. Small single-truck Birney cars were assigned to this rural line in 1920, but uneven track gave a rough ride, and passengers complained. In 1921, Birneys were replaced with seven of these modern double-truck steel trolleys. These served the Bristol-to-Doylestown line for only two years before trolley service was canceled in 1923. (Courtesy of the Norman Kitchin collection, Newtown Historic Association.)

Car No. 7 turns from Bridge Street onto South Main Street in New Hope. Having just crossed the Delaware River bridge from Lambertville, its destination is Trenton, 16 miles distant. The sign in the front window reminds passengers that they may also transfer to Newtown trolleys. The transfer point was at Yardley. The rails extending to the left were constructed in 1915 to provide access to a new trolley freight terminal. (Courtesy of Steven Cohen.)

Trolley track in the borough of New Hope was placed at the edge of the street against the curb, unlike most towns in which trolley tracks occupied the center of the streets. This c. 1906 view finds car No. 2 moving south on South Main Street past the New Hope Methodist Episcopal Church. The imposing stone building stands today although it no longer serves as a house of worship. (Courtesy of the Pennsylvania Trolley Museum.)

This southbound trolley on South Main Street in New Hope passes locks Nos. 10 and 11 of the Delaware Division of the Pennsylvania Canal. Just beyond the right edge of this view, both Main Street and the trolley track curve sharply and cross over a bridge to the west side of the canal. (Courtesy of the Pennsylvania Trolley Museum.)

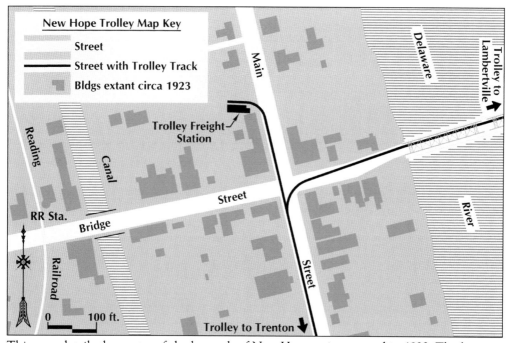

This map details the center of the borough of New Hope as it appeared in 1923. The location of the trolley freight station shown here is likely but has not been conclusively determined. A Sanborn insurance map made after the trolley line was abandoned in 1924 labels the building as "storage." (Drafted by the author.)

Trolleys from Trenton passed through New Hope and ended their trips across the Delaware River in Lambertville, New Jersey. This July 26, 1906, view captures car No. 1 at the end of the trolley track on Bridge Street at Lambert Lane in Lambertville. The single-track Belvidere Delaware steam railroad and the Delaware and Raritan feeder canal are immediately behind the photographer. (Courtesy of the Pennsylvania Trolley Museum.)

Passengers wait for their turn to board Trenton-bound car No. 7 on Bridge Street in Lambertville. The ride to Yardley was scheduled to take 30 minutes; Trenton was reached in 50 minutes. All except the building at far left still stand. The address of the building at right is 6 Bridge Street, Lambertville, New Jersey. (Courtesy of the Stephen D. Maguire collection, James C. McHugh.)

Excitement ran high as the first trolley crossed the Delaware River on June 15, 1905. This photograph taken on the New Jersey side shows the extremely tight clearance between the electric current collection pole atop the car and the steel framework of the through-truss bridge. This bridge was nearly new, having replaced a wooden covered bridge destroyed in a 1903 flood. (Courtesy of James C. McHugh.)

Car No. 11 has derailed, striking a stone wall supporting a canal lock and severing a wooden utility pole on South Main Street in New Hope. The man wearing the apron at left is identified as Thomas J. Walker. The identity of the boy in the white shirt standing in the doorway is not known, but the man standing next to him is John Pickett. The man at far right is Thomas Knealy. (Courtesy of the Pennsylvania Trolley Museum.)

Long stretches of the trolley line between Yardley and New Hope left the roadside and ran on railroad-style private right-of-way. Portions of the line included significant rock excavation, as can be seen in this c. 1906 view. A 90-foot-long steel through-truss bridge enabled the trolley line to span Pidcock Creek near the Thompson-Neely house and Bowman's Hill. (Courtesy of Andrew W. Maginnis.)

Curious residents stand in the side yard of 1502 River Road in Upper Makefield Township watching a photographer's attempt to capture a trolley as it speeds toward Trenton. This house still stands on the east side of River Road north of the intersection with Brownsburg Road East. (Courtesy of Steven Cohen.)

Heavy, wet snow was more than a match for trolley plows, and on occasion, scores of men and boys had to be hired to dig out the trolley lines. This 1920 photograph was taken at Scammell's Corner in Lower Makefield Township. Yardley lay half a mile away at the foot of the long Afton Avenue hill. Houses barely visible to the right of the barn are along Sandy Run Road. (Courtesy of Yardley Historical Association.)

With its destination sign displaying simply FREIGHT, this former passenger trolley slips between snowbanks nearly as high as its roof. A February 1920 blizzard was particularly brutal, with drifts reported to be as deep as 10 feet. At the height of the storm, mail carrier Horace P. Atkinson perished in a snowdrift while carrying a mailbag to the Wycombe Post Office. (Courtesy of Newtown Historic Association.)

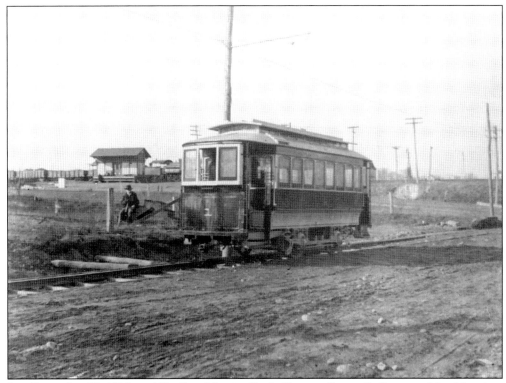

It is December 27, 1900, and Yardley, Morrisville & Trenton Street Railway car No. 1 has just been placed on new rails along South Main Street in Yardley. Car No. 1 was purchased used from the Lehigh Valley Traction Company of Allentown. The Main Street underpass beneath the Reading Railroad is outside the right edge of this view. Reading Railroad's Yardley freight station is visible in the distance. (Courtesy of the Pennsylvania Trolley Museum.)

Yardley's Continental Tavern has presided over the corner of Afton Avenue and Main Street since 1877. Trolley tracks linking Newtown and Trenton were laid around this corner in 1903; the location became a trolley junction when the line to New Hope and Lambertville opened in 1905. It is possible that the large turnout of townspeople in this postcard view was due to the inaugural run of the New Hope line on June 15, 1905. (Courtesy of the Pennsylvania Trolley Museum.)

Trolley freight car No. 60 is southbound on Main Street in Yardley. The photographer has set his tripod at Letchworth Avenue. The house on the left stands at 165 South Main Street. After the trolley lines north and west of Yardley were abandoned in 1924, this trolley was sold to Hershey Transit Company. Enough remained of the network of interconnecting trolley lines for this trolley to be run on trolley tracks the entire 120 miles to Hershey, Pennsylvania. (Courtesy of Yardley Historical Association.)

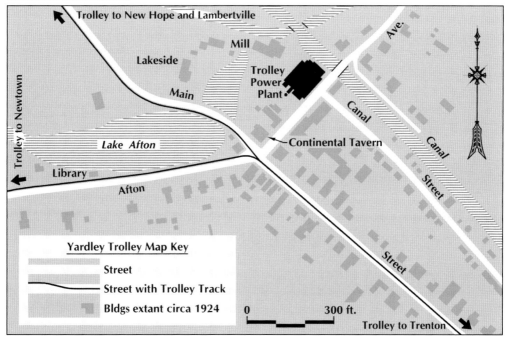

The layout of trolley tracks in Yardley is depicted on this map. The track on Afton Street was not used after 1924. The track on Main Street was used by electric streetcars running from McKinley Avenue through Morrisville to Trenton until September 1934. (Drafted by the author.)

This Trenton-to-Newtown trolley is leaving Yardley, about to cross the trolley bridge over Brock Creek along Afton Avenue. The stone trolley bridge abutments stood until 1960, when they were demolished by the Pennsylvania Department of Highways to make room for a new, wider Afton Avenue Bridge. Both houses stand today, at 85 and 93 West Afton Avenue. (Courtesy of Newtown Historic Association.)

Tragedy struck on Wednesday, July 23, 1913, when a runaway trolley, unable to make the sharp curve from Afton Avenue onto Main Street, overturned. Trolley car No. 8 lost its brakes descending Nickleson's hill west of town and could not be stopped. Just as the speeding trolley entered the corner, passenger Thomas Rose of Yardley leapt from an open door but lost his life beneath the overturned car. (Courtesy of the Pennsylvania Trolley Museum.)

Of the seven modern steel trolley cars purchased in 1921, five were sold to the Binghamton, New York, trolley system when the lines beyond Yardley were abandoned, and two were retained for Trenton-to-Yardley service. No. 125 is northbound after passing beneath the Reading Railroad in Yardley. The curb curving to the right leads into Reading Avenue. Wide open front windows suggest this July 1934 day was a warm one. (Photograph by William H. Watts II.)

Seen here in 1940 after it was decommissioned, this powerhouse at 16 East Afton Avenue in Yardley once generated electric power for a far-flung trolley system that stretched from Doylestown and Bristol to Princeton, New Jersey. In June 1923, the traction company found it cheaper to purchase power from Philadelphia Suburban Gas and Electric Company, and the plant was downgraded to a substation. Today, this building serves as the home of Cramer's Bakery and a CVS pharmacy. (Courtesy of Yardley Historical Association.)

Pennsylvania–New Jersey Railway car No. 125 squeals around a tight curve from Mill Street onto the Calhoun Street Bridge in Morrisville on January 30, 1932. The Trenton State House dome gleams across the Delaware River in Trenton. Painted red, this trolley was one of seven purchased in 1921 from the Perley A. Thomas Car Works of High Point, North Carolina. The company today builds school buses under the name Thomas Built. (Courtesy of James C. McHugh.)

Perhaps the most eccentric piece of rolling stock to carry passengers in lower Bucks County was this secondhand Brooklyn Rapid Transit Company parlor car. With its vast plateglass side windows, the car was built by J.G. Brill in 1898 for the Brooklyn & Coney Island Railroad. In 1927, PA-NJ management decided to purchase this trolley and convert the interior for regular passenger service. The building with the mansard roof above the trolley is 21 North Pennsylvania Avenue, Morrisville. (Courtesy of James C. McHugh.)

It is July 15, 1934, and Birney car No. 20 is performing Morrisville Loop duties. The location is Mill Street, today known as Delmorr Drive (see page 74 for a map of Morrisville). The light weight of the Birney car coupled with a design intended to be operated by one man without a conductor made them popular with cost-conscious trolley systems. When first delivered in 1920, the public derisively referred to Birneys as "cheese box" cars. (Photograph by William H. Watts II.)

The Calhoun Street Bridge over the Delaware River was erected in 1884 by the Phoenix Bridge Company of Phoenixville, Pennsylvania. The seven through-truss spans are built of wrought iron rather than steel. Trolley track was laid on the south side of the deck in 1901. In 1913, the Lincoln Highway was routed over this bridge; trolleys moving both directions in the eastbound lane meant that every other trolley was "bucking traffic." Trolley service over the bridge ended in 1934, and the rails were removed in 1940. (Courtesy of the Pennsylvania Trolley Museum.)

Three trolleys await departure at the West Hanover Street terminal in Trenton on May 23, 1934. Trolley car No. 22 (left) is bound for Princeton on the Princeton Fast Line. Car No. 125 (center) will cross the Calhoun Street Bridge and, after a quarter mile on Trenton Avenue, will turn north for Yardley. Car No. 20 (right) will also cross the Calhoun Street Bridge and head west on Trenton Avenue but will turn south and make the Morrisville Loop. (Courtesy of James C. McHugh.)

Only a few months of trolley service remained as PA-NJ car No. 125 from Trenton approached the waiting shelter at Edgewood Road on Yardley Morrisville Road in Lower Makefield Township. The date is May 23, 1934. Without approval from either the New Jersey or the Pennsylvania Public Utility Commissions, trolley service came to an end on September 2, 1934. Overhead wires were removed in 1935, but trolley tracks remained embedded in some streets for many years. (Courtesy of the Stephen D. Maguire collection, Andrew W. Maginnis.)

Four

BENSALEM, BRISTOL, MORRISVILLE

TROLLEYS ON THE KING'S HIGHWAY

Philadelphia, Bristol & Trenton (PB&T) cars Nos. 26 and 25 meet at a passing siding on Bristol Pike between Croydon and West Bristol. Much of this trolley line was built on the old colonial road once known as the King's Highway. Beginning at the Philadelphia city line at Andalusia, through Croydon and Bristol to Morrisville, construction of the various segments occurred over seven years, beginning in 1896. Trackage rights over Pennsylvania–New Jersey Railway gave the trolleys access to downtown Trenton. Gasoline buses phased out the electric streetcars between 1929 and 1932. (Courtesy of the Pennsylvania Trolley Museum.)

This charming scene presented itself to those about to leave Philadelphia and cross into Bucks County at Andalusia around 1905. The vantage point is the new concrete bridge over Poquessing Creek. Beyond the trolley bearing the destination sign BRISTOL lies the Red Lion Inn. Dating to 1730, the storied Red Lion was one of the earliest establishments in the Pennsylvania colony. Favored as a meeting place during the Revolutionary War, a 1991 fire gutted the historic tavern, and it was not rebuilt. (Courtesy of Robert Homolka.)

Frankford, Tacony & Holmesburg (FT&H) Street Railway's tracks occupied Frankford Avenue and State Road in Northeast Philadelphia. FT&H rails connected with those of the PB&T at the city/county boundary on the bridge over Poquessing Creek in Andalusia. In the early years, rather than force riders to transfer between trolley cars, the cooperating companies through-routed trolleys between Bristol and Frankford. FT&H open car No. 39 is about to depart Otter Street in Bristol, bound for Bridge Street in Frankford. (Courtesy of Steven Cohen.)

An early single-truck trolley comes around "the S bend" on Bristol Pike at Eddington in about 1910. The photographer is facing south. The stone bridge to the right provided access to the St. Francis Industrial School for Boys property. A railroad siding to the school crossed the highway and the trolley track at grade just beyond the bend. In Bensalem Township, the trolley track was located in the middle of the road even before the highway was paved with concrete in the 1920s. (Courtesy of Robert Homolka.)

One horseless carriage and Frankford, Tacony & Holmesburg open car No. 17 have the road to themselves in Andalusia on this warm summer day. During the early years, the tracks were forced to detour off Bristol Pike for a short distance because permission could not be obtained from owners of properties fronting the road. This view looks north between Tennis Avenue and Richardson Avenue. The house at left still stands at 922 Bristol Pike, Bensalem Township. (Courtesy of the Pennsylvania Trolley Museum.)

This steel pony truss bridge over Neshaminy Creek, designed for trolleys on the downstream side and vehicle traffic on the other, was built by the trolley company in 1897. It replaced an earlier wooden bridge that was deemed insufficient to support the weight of trolley cars. The open trolley is car No. 31 of the Frankford, Tacony & Holmesburg Street Railway Company on its way to Bristol. (Courtesy of the Pennsylvania Trolley Museum.)

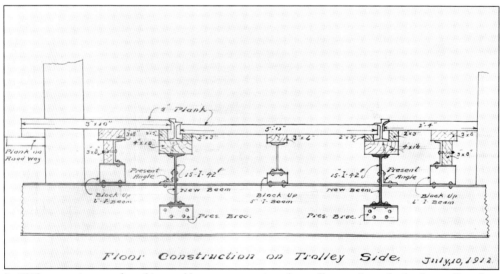

In 1912, corrosion was found in steel beams supporting the trolley track on the bridge at Croydon. Because agreement could not be reached between Bucks County and the trolley company regarding the cost of repairs, a court order blocked trolleys from using the bridge, with passengers forced to disembark and walk across. This situation persisted from July to December 1912. Repairs were designed by the office of Doylestown architect and engineer A. Oscar Martin. (Courtesy of the collection of the Mercer Museum, Bucks County Historical Society.)

An ice jam threatens the trolley bridge over Neshaminy Creek at Croydon in this late 1890s view. The open trolleys so common in early photographs have been mothballed for the winter, with closed cars equipped with stoves carrying passengers for the season. The trolley powerhouse with its smoke stack can be seen on the north bank of the creek. The embankment to the right supports the Pennsylvania Railroad's four-track Philadelphia–to–New York line. (Courtesy of the Pennsylvania Trolley Museum.)

A cloud of steam vents from the side of the Croydon trolley powerhouse on the north bank of Neshaminy Creek. A three-track carbarn adjoins the east wall of the power plant. The plant's coal supply was brought up the creek by barge. The vantage point is trackside on the Pennsylvania Railroad approach to the railroad bridge over Neshaminy Creek. This portion of Bristol Pike was abandoned when the new highway was constructed a hundred yards to the north, behind these buildings. (Courtesy of the Pennsylvania Trolley Museum.)

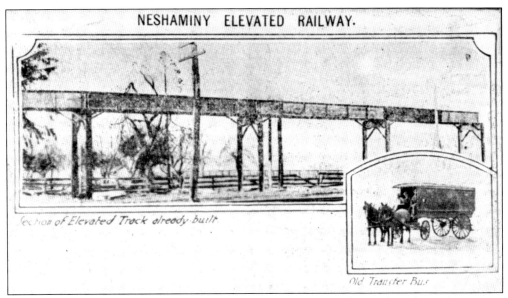

NESHAMINY ELEVATED RAILWAY.

Section of Elevated Track already built.

Old Transfer Bus

In Pennsylvania, trolley lines were not permitted to occupy public roads without the written permission of the owners of property fronting the road. Trolleys often crossed from one side of the road to the other, depending on which property owner was more amenable. In cases where both property owners withheld permission, trouble ensued. Such was the case north of Croydon along Bristol Pike. The Pennsylvania Railroad on one side and a Mr. Gaw on the other both refused to allow trolley construction. When the state legislature passed a law granting elevated railroads the right of eminent domain, the trolley promoters saw an opportunity (the legislation was intended to enable construction of the Market Street Elevated in Philadelphia). In 1902, a short section of single-track elevated railway was built at Croydon (above) without the long ramps that would have actually made it useful. In 1903, after seven long years, the trolley track was laid along Bristol Pike, and the horse-drawn buses used to ferry passengers (below) were no longer needed. (Above, courtesy of Andrew W. Maginnis; below, courtesy of James C. McHugh.)

Trenton, Philadelphia & Bristol Street Railway Company owned an assortment of used trolley cars in the early years. Car No. 24, with its drooping body evidently too long for its short-wheelbase four-wheel truck, was likely purchased secondhand from the Baltimore, Maryland, street railway system. Barker Gummere identified the location as Otter Street, and two of the three crewmen are Jesse Keene (center) and Frank Delid (right). (Courtesy of the Pennsylvania Trolley Museum.)

A Philadelphia-bound trolley approaches the bridge over Martins Creek in Tullytown. The view looks north on Main Street from the intersection with Manor Avenue. In the century since this photograph was taken, the main span over the creek has been replaced, but the stone parapet walls of the approaches are still in place. A datestone on the left bears the date 1901. (Courtesy of James C. McHugh.)

Car No. 15 was representative of the classic Brill semi-convertible car popular in the first years of the 20th century. Rather than simply open a window in warm weather, the upper and lower sashes of a semi-convertible trolley could be folded up into pockets built into the ceiling, rewarding passengers with the unimpeded views and refreshing breezes of an open car. By the time of this c. 1910 photograph, the company had been reorganized as the Trenton, Bristol & Philadelphia Street Railway Company. (Courtesy of the Pennsylvania Trolley Museum.)

Mill Street is the commercial heart of Bristol Borough. This view looks north from the intersection with Radcliffe Street. The Delaware River waterfront with its wharves and ferry terminal are one block behind the photographer. Note the bicycle and rider to the right of the track. A single trolley track in the middle of the street, with trolleys moving both directions on it, left plenty of space for all road users in the era before parked automobiles assumed the right to block the curbside lanes. (Courtesy of James C. McHugh.)

TB&P No. 15—the same trolley at the top of the opposite page—rolls north on Radcliffe Street near the intersection with Franklin Street in Bristol on its way to Trenton, New Jersey. Because this and sister car No. 14 were acquired in 1903 and would be resold to the Chambersburg-Shippensburg trolley line in 1914, this photograph must have been taken between those years. The address of the house on the left is 515 Radcliffe Street. (Courtesy of Andrew W. Maginnis.)

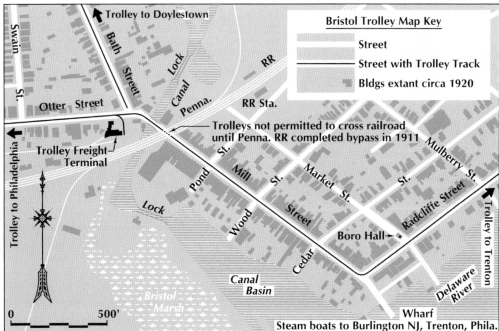

The layout of trolley tracks in Bristol is depicted on this map. The early railroad track that was laid the length of Market Street in the 1830s is not shown. The office and waiting room of the trolley company occupied space in the building on the east corner of Radcliffe and Market Streets. (Drafted by the author.)

July 24, 1921, was a somber day in Bristol as the remains of World War I veteran Robert W. Bracken were laid to rest at Bristol Cemetery. The 26-year-old Bracken was the first Bristol casualty of the war, killed in the Battle of St. Mihiel in France in 1918. American Legion Post No. 382 was formed on September 28, 1919, and named in Bracken's honor. The view above looks west from atop the Pennsylvania Railroad overpass over Bristol Pike as mourners enter the gates of Bristol Cemetery. The view below looks east (toward Bristol) from that same bridge. The trolley accompanying the funeral procession, presumably carrying those not able to walk the mile from town, is either car No. 22 or 23. In the years after these photographs were taken, the highway was paved with concrete, and the trolley track was relocated from the south shoulder of the road to the north side. The location of the passing siding beneath the bridge was also moved. (Both, courtesy of the Pennsylvania Trolley Museum.)

This R.C. Maxwell billboard company photograph was taken on October 10, 1932. By this time, only one trolley trip was scheduled each day, a so-called "franchise run" so that it could not be said that the trolley line was officially replaced with buses. Leaning support poles mean the end is near. The location is Old Bristol Pike in Falls Township, one mile south of the intersection of Philadelphia and Pennsylvania Avenues in Morrisville. (Courtesy of R.C. Maxwell Co. Records, David M. Rubenstein Rare Book & Manuscript Library, Duke University.)

This October 26, 1931, photograph of the yard at Croydon barn was taken during the time when motor buses had replaced most trolley runs. Detailed notes made by Howard E. Johnston relate that old railroad-roof car No. 23 (left) was painted blue (it had been green) and that it had been purchased secondhand in 1919 from the Milford, Attleboro & Woonsocket Street Railway of Massachusetts. Birney car No. 46 (center) was painted red. The color of line car No. 45 (right) was not recorded. (Courtesy of the Pennsylvania Trolley Museum.)

In 1914, large steel trolleys were ordered from the J.G. Brill company of Philadelphia (above). Their capacity was put to good use carrying workers to the Merchant Shipbuilding Corporation shipyard at Harriman during World War I. Because the five-car fleet was resold to the Altoona & Logan Valley Electric Railway in 1920, few photographs survive. The postcard view below shows one of these trolleys southbound on Radcliffe Street at Jefferson Street in Bristol. In September 1914, the company advised that, with the new trolleys, the following new rules were in effect: "Passengers are to enter the car at the right hand side and the front of car," and "the exit door is at the front left hand side." In addition, "[the company] will not be able to take ice cream tubs or large boxes on the car. Small, clean packages will be carried on the cars as at present, but no large packages will be taken." Those were to be carried on board daily scheduled freight trolleys. (Above, courtesy of the Pennsylvania Trolley Museum; below, courtesy of James C. McHugh.)

A small fleet of six Brill-built Birney "safety cars" arrived in January 1920. Their limited capacity was offset by their modest power consumption, which saved the company money, and the fact that they could be operated by one man without a conductor. The industry term "safety car" was intended to allay fears that the new design might be prone to accidents because the motorman was tasked with the duties of a two-man crew. The *Bristol Daily Courier* dubbed them "cheese box" cars. (Courtesy of the Margaret R. Grundy Memorial Library.)

Two more Birney cars were acquired secondhand from the Milford & Uxbridge Street Railway of Massachusetts in 1927. Seen here wearing a bold paint scheme, No. 21 was repainted all red in later years. Since 1924, the TB&P controlled the PA-NJ (see chapter three), and car No. 21 was assigned to the Morrisville carbarn, assigned to Trenton runs. Car No. 21 made the final run over the Calhoun Street Bridge, returning to the Morrisville barn one last time at 1:50 a.m. on September 2, 1934. (Courtesy of the Pennsylvania Trolley Museum.)

This evocative 1920s image finds a TB&P Birney car southbound on Bristol Pike in Eddington during a snowfall. The camera is pointed north along Bristol Pike from present-day Gibbs Road. Because heavy, wet snow plastering the front of the trolley could impede the motorman's view, he needed to stop at intervals to clean the windshield. Automobiles built in 1920 were not required to be equipped with windshield wipers, and neither were trolley cars. (Courtesy of the Historical Society of Bensalem Township.)

New communities enabled by affordable and convenient rapid transit were referred to as "streetcar suburbs." This c. 1920 view frames a TB&P trolley along Bristol Pike and a new residential development. The white columns bracket the entrance to Bristol Cemetery. The billboard reading "For sale: small farms, houses, building lots, West Bristol" stood at the corner of Newport and Old Rodgers Roads. The house to the left of the sign still stands at 206 Newport Road, Bristol. (Courtesy of the Pennsylvania Trolley Museum.)

A TB&P Birney car pauses on gravel Bristol Pike at Cornwells Avenue in Bensalem Township. In 1925, TB&P was ordered to rebuild its track so the highway could be paved with concrete. General manager Minot J. Hill asked the state to do the track work and offered to reimburse by paying $60,000 over 20 years. Unimpressed, state highway department official W.H. Connell called that "the most extraordinary offer the department has ever received from a street railway company." An agreement was eventually hammered out. (Courtesy of the Historical Society of Bensalem Township.)

This June 12, 1928, photograph was taken to document unsafe conditions at a trolley highway crossing south of Edgely. The view looks north from the intersection of North Radcliffe and Hammond Streets. The tracks would be adjusted to move the crossing to a point 300 feet south where there were better sight lines. The address of the house on the left is 6831 Radcliffe Street, Bristol. (Courtesy of the collection of the Mercer Museum, Bucks County Historical Society.)

Growing up in the 1920s, William H. Watts II was intrigued by the trolley cars that rolled through his Chestnut Hill neighborhood in Philadelphia. His interest soon expanded to include the trolley lines outside the city. During the winter of 1931–1932, Watts made several trips to ride and photograph the TB&P trolley line from Andalusia, through Bristol, to Morrisville. The photographs on this and the facing page are ones he took on those occasions. On February 13, 1932 (above), a PRT Route 66 trolley on Frankford Avenue reaches the end of the line on the Philadelphia side of the bridge at Andalusia. Passengers could continue their trip north by boarding TB&P car No. 43 waiting on the Bucks County side. On December 5, 1931 (below), car No. 43 pauses at the Croydon powerhouse. (Both, photographs by William H. Watts II, courtesy of the Pennsylvania Trolley Museum.)

TB&P car No. 43 is northbound heading toward Bristol on Otter Street, then designated US Route 13. The date is Saturday, February 14, 1932. The overhead plate-girder bridge carrying the four-track Pennsylvania Railroad over the highway was built during the 1911 Bristol grade-separation project. Resourceful shop crews have fitted the 12-year-old Birney car with mismatched wooden doors salvaged from an older trolley. (Photograph by William H. Watts II, courtesy of Richard Allman.)

South-facing TB&P car No. 43 is on Pennsylvania Avenue at Bridge Street in Morrisville on February 13, 1932. In later years, with both track and trolleys in rough shape, some referred to the TB&P as the Torn, Broken & Patched. Once a major employer, the brick Vulcanized Rubber plant closed in 1980 and was later razed. Today, Robert Morris Plaza with its seven-foot-high bronze statue of Robert Morris occupies the corner behind the trolley car. (Photograph by William H. Watts II, courtesy of Richard Allman.)

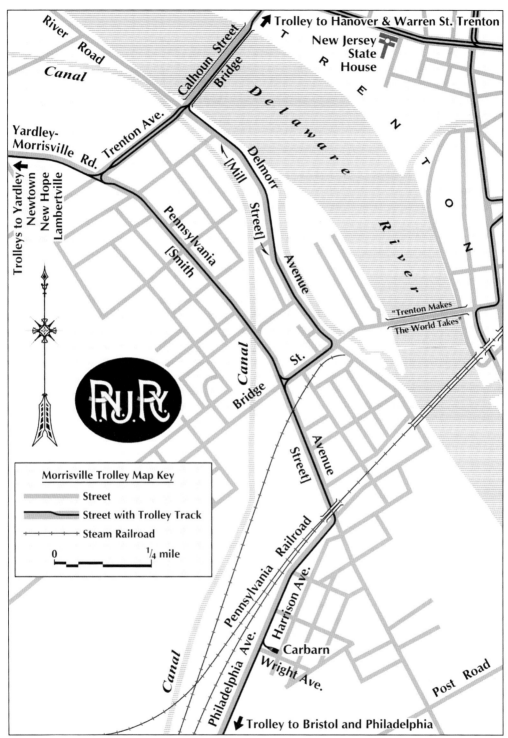

This map shows the tracks of the PA-NJ and the TB&P trolley systems in Morrisville. After 1924, TB&P management controlled both systems. The "P.N.J. Ry." logo seen here was painted on the sides of the Perley Thomas streetcars that arrived in 1921. (Drafted by the author.)

Trolley plow No. 41, with its blade crusted with snow, rests in the Morrisville carbarn. A sign in the cab reads, "Plows Must Be Raised 9" To Clear Calhoun St. Bridge." The three-track corrugated metal carbarn was erected in 1924 at Wright and Harrison Avenues. By the end of service, the building was run down. Lack of doors where the tracks entered must have made for grim working conditions for mechanics in winter. (Courtesy of James C. McHugh.)

Taken four years after the trolleys last ran, this May 1938 view looks east on Bridge Street from Pennsylvania Avenue, capturing the tidy business district with the tracks still in the street. Trolley wire had been cut down in 1935. Trolleys from Trenton entered the intersection from the left; those bound for Trenton went straight ahead on Bridge Street. Trolleys to and from Bristol and Philadelphia used the track on the right. (Courtesy of R.C. Maxwell Co. Records, David M. Rubenstein Rare Book & Manuscript Library, Duke University.)

Delaware River Coach Company was TB&P's bus division. The buses gradually took over trolley runs between 1929 and 1932. Here, a bus is tasked with pulling derailed line car No. 45 back onto the track. Bus and trolley are headed north, north of Bristol. The workman is standing on Landreth Lane. The Tudor-style house glimpsed through the trees at left is 6420 Radcliffe Street, Bristol Township. (Courtesy of James C. McHugh.)

After the end of trolley service between Morrisville and Philadelphia, these Birney cars were scrapped at Croydon carbarn. Tipping over the cars facilitated removal of equipment that could be recycled or resold. As it turned out, running buses instead of trolleys did not end the company's troubles. In 1935, the state public service commission ordered Delaware River Coach buses off the streets, awarding the franchise instead to competitor Neibauer Bus Company. (Courtesy of the Pennsylvania Trolley Museum.)

Five

DOYLESTOWN, PLUMSTEADVILLE, RIEGELSVILLE

ROAD OF WILD ROSES

Northbound Doylestown & Easton Street Railway Company car No. 3's passengers lean out open windows on Old Easton Road above Danboro. The narrow bridge crosses North Branch Neshaminy Creek. Built between 1901 and 1904, this 32-mile trolley line had been reorganized as the Philadelphia & Easton Railway in 1903. The power for this line was generated at the hydroelectric Clymer power plant on the Delaware Canal south of Raubsville in Northampton County. A coal fired plant in Raubsville (still standing) served as a backup. The last day for these trolleys was Thanksgiving Day 1926. (Courtesy of Andrew W. Maginnis.)

D&E car No. 5 bound for Easton meets a Philadelphia Rapid Transit Company open car headed to Willow Grove. Although the D&E's tracks extended over Court and Clinton Streets to the Reading Railroad station, most trolley runs ended here on Main Street north of Monument Square. Running a small shuttle car over the Court and Clinton Streets tracks was tried for a time, but the light patronage did not justify the expense. (Courtesy of Andrew W. Maginnis.)

This April 1908 photograph captures both the D&E office building, with its first-floor waiting room, and the old Bucks County Courthouse. The location is the east side of North Main Street between Court and Broad Streets. Easton and Willow Grove trolleys met here and, after 1910, Bristol trolleys as well. Before the trolley company purchased it, a Sanborn insurance map identified the building as a two-story gymnasium and reading room. (Courtesy of the Solebury Township Historical Society.)

Doylestown & Easton combination passenger–and–railway post office car No. 11 and freight motor No. 100 occupy the curbside track at the D&E trolley station on North Main Street. In 1910, D&E agreed to share its tracks, enabling Philadelphia trolley freight cars to access a new freight station on Union Street (see map on page 14). After PRT canceled trolley freight service in 1922, D&E extended trolley track into the Reading Company yard on South Clinton Street to facilitate the transfer of freight. (Courtesy of Steven Cohen.)

In July 1901, the Mercer family refused to allow trolley tracks on Main Street north of Old Dublin Pike. Because the Mercers owned property on both sides of the road, a costly detour had to be built on Lacey Avenue, North Street, and private right-of-way. The Mercers relented and allowed tracks to be built along the road in 1907. This c. 1916 view looks north on Main Street from the bridge over Cook's Run. (Courtesy of the collection of the Mercer Museum, Bucks County Historical Society.)

This snowy scene finds D&E car No. 11 headed north in Plumsteadville. The location is Easton Road at Stump Road. The wooden waiting platform has been thoroughly cleared of snow. A sign above the platform reads, "Electric Car Station." In later years, a wood-frame waiting shelter was erected nearby. The Plumsteadville Inn (just outside the right edge of the photograph) was once known as the Redrock Tavern and dates to colonial times. (Courtesy of Stanley F. Bowman Jr.)

One of the D&E trolley's greatest advocates was Plumsteadville entrepreneur Aaron Kratz. His carriage works employed 50 men over many years. Sought after for their high quality, Kratz carriages, sleighs, and wagons were sold across the eastern United States and Canada. Kratz invested heavily in the trolley line—$100,000 ($3 million in 2020 dollars). Late in his life, as the D&E was struggling, he was asked about his decision to invest nearly his entire fortune in the trolley. He replied that he had no regrets, adding "I believe I have done my duty to Bucks County." The image at left dates to 1901; the advertisement is from 1898. (Author's collection.)

Single-truck D&E car No. 10 occupies one of two tracks in front of the Plumsteadville carbarn. Built in 1902, the carbarn was described as "a frame building with galvanized iron roof, 30 by 85 feet, has one pit and will hold four cars." The temporary coal-fired electrical plant behind the barn was only used until October 1904, when power was sent down the line from Northampton County. A new building now occupies this site at 5995 Easton Road, Plumstead Township. (Courtesy of Steven Cohen.)

A curious child watches the photographer work on Old Easton Road at Curly Hill Road, midway between Danboro and Plumsteadville. This north-facing view reveals the condition of the roads before improvements were made. The electric trolley running on smooth steel rails was a marvelous convenience to those living and working along the line. A trackside brick electrical substation building located behind the photographer no longer stands today. Its precise location is documented on 1920s state highway department drawings. (Courtesy of Stanley F. Bowman Jr.)

This postcard view shows a stone arch bridge for a farm road that leads to 6330 Easton Road in Bedminster Township, north of Plumsteadville. In the distance, northbound D&E car No. 101, built for carrying hay bales, can be seen on the track that paralleled Easton Road. Located on private property, the stone bridge is still in place in 2020. (Courtesy of Steven Cohen.)

This broad, well-trod footpath led from the Pipersville trolley station to the village crossroads and the Pipersville Inn. When the trolley was surveyed, rather than run through the center of Pipersville, the track made a three-quarter-mile detour through the fields west of town. In January 1906, Pipersville Inn proprietor Cyrus Raub brought suit alleging that the trolley company reneged on a promise to provide lighting for this walkway in exchange for right-of-way. (Courtesy of Steven Cohen.)

Labels on postcards are not always accurate, and such seems to be the case with this sharp real-photo postcard of D&E crewmen with southbound car No. 2, photographed by Linford Craven of Doylestown. The location is the bridge over Deep Run just north of Pipersville. Plumsteadville is three miles south of this bridge. The parallel Easton Road crossing of Deep Run can be glimpsed behind the trolley bridge. (Courtesy of Steven Cohen.)

D&E crewmen stand for the photographer with passenger car No. 6 (left) and a work car (right). The work car is likely No. 102. This small, four-wheel trolley had been purchased secondhand from Philadelphia Rapid Transit Company in 1904 to shuttle passengers between Ottsville and Ferndale when the electrical system was not yet up to the task of powering larger cars. Finishing out its years as a drop-side gondola, it had started out as a Philadelphia horsecar. (Courtesy of the John Gibb Smith collection, James C. McHugh.)

In 1905, the D&E took delivery of a new trolley freight car. Built by the Jackson & Sharp Company of Wilmington, Delaware, car No. 100 moved all manner of goods, including milk cans, for 20 years until the cancellation of trolley freight service in 1925. Although details about the origins of this photograph have not come to light, those pictured are identified as members of the Trumbore family. (Courtesy of David F. Drinkhouse.)

Car No. 101 is unique among trolley cars in that it was specifically designed to haul hay bales. The car's open sides facilitated loading and unloading. Close inspection of this 1909 builder's photograph, taken at the J.G. Brill Company plant in Southwest Philadelphia, reveals striped canvas curtains rolled up against the roof. These were intended to be deployed during inclement weather in an effort to keep the cargo dry. (Courtesy of Andrew W. Maginnis.)

Many trolley lines carried mail on a daily basis for the US Post Office, but the Doylestown & Easton was one of the few in Pennsylvania to operate a railway post office (RPO). In July 1905, two combination passenger-and-baggage cars, Nos. 11 and 12, were placed in service. Built by the Jackson & Sharp Company, the baggage compartment was fitted with everything required for a postal employee to sort mail en route. After the RPO contract was canceled on April 1, 1908, the trolleys were operated under their own power to the J.G. Brill Plant in Southwest Philadelphia, where the mail-sorting apparatus was removed and replaced with seats for passengers. (Above, courtesy of Stanley F. Bowman Jr.; below, courtesy of the Barker Gummere collection, James C. McHugh.)

Even before the trolley line was completed, the D&E invited visitors to company-owned 153-acre Tohickon Park. During the spring and summer of 1903, a horse-drawn hack conveyed trolley passengers the final mile and a half from Pipersville. Attractions included a creek-side picnic grove and a dance pavilion. Picnic tables and what appear to be swings can be seen through the stone arches. D&E No. 4 is southbound on the Easton Road Bridge over Tohickon Creek. (Courtesy of Steven Cohen.)

Southbound freight motor No. 100 exchanges cargo with a teamster's wagon at the south end of the Easton Road Bridge over Tohickon Creek. Tohickon Park is behind the photographer. Referring to the 1737 Walking Purchase, in 1905, historian William Davis wrote, "Teedyuscung, the great Delaware king, frequently declared the Tohickon to be the northern limit of the white man's country, and that lands to the north of it had been taken from them fraudulently." (Courtesy of James C. McHugh.)

Crewmen have climbed down from northbound D&E car No. 1 and stand before the Old Red Hill Tavern on Easton Road north of Ottsville. Published in a trolley guidebook, the caption reads, "Built before the Revolution. Full of Indian Relics. Can be seen by calling on James Emery." The historic inn was demolished when Easton Road was realigned. The stone Walking Purchase monument visible at right was relocated nearby. (Courtesy of Steven Cohen.)

Southbound D&E car No. 3 stands before 244 Durham Road in the village of Ottsville, Tinicum Township. As the trolley lines were being laid out, the designers were sometimes forced to switch which side of the road they built the track on, depending on how amenable property owners on opposite sides of the road were. In Ottsville, the trolley track crossed and recrossed the road twice over a short distance. This photograph captures car No. 3 on the track between the crossings. (Courtesy of David F. Drinkhouse.)

An early automobile follows a northbound D&E trolley on Easton Road between Revere and Ferndale. This view gives a good sense of the ill-defined boundary between the roadway and the trolley track in the years before the road was paved with concrete. Sharp curves, or as in this view, an abrupt hilltop crest, could present a motorist with an oncoming trolley and not much time to react. The house on the left still stands at 9040 Easton Road in Nockamixon Township. (Courtesy of Andrew W. Maginnis.)

Trolleys were scheduled to meet at Revere Siding in Nockamixon Township, located directly across the street from Nockamixon Consolidated School (today's Schoolhouse Apartments). The motormen's names were not recorded, but the conductor standing second from left is Ben Fleming, and the conductor at right is Oscar Stone. Located midway between Doylestown and Easton, this was also known as Center Switch. (Courtesy of the collection of Jean Fleming Frankenfield, David F. Drinkhouse.)

This 1920s view finds a southbound D&E trolley on the left side of the Ferndale Inn, with the new concrete state highway on the right. The trolley track crossed and recrossed the road's old alignment twice over a short distance in Ferndale. The new 18-foot-wide concrete highway built in 1921 was steeper but was also straighter and bypassed both trolley crossings. Reducing grade-crossing collisions was a priority as motor vehicle traffic volumes and speeds increased. (Courtesy of Nockamixon Township Historical Commission.)

Trolley freight motor No. 100 (lower right) stops at a freight platform at Sunnyside Truck Farm in Nockamixon Township. Arrow-straight Ealer Hill Road leads off to the west (along the left edge). A c. 1905 trolley guidebook lavished the following praise: "None of the hundreds of fine farms along the line are more beautiful or better kept than this one. Mr. W. O. Ealer supplies the city of Easton with many of its finest vegetables. His place shows how attractive a farm may be made." (Courtesy of James C. McHugh.)

Easton-bound D&E car No. 1 is stopped on the bridge over Gallow's Run south of Kintnersville. The intersection of Easton Road and Kintner Hill Road is just beyond the right edge of the view. Six trolleys of this design were built by John Stephenson Car Company of Elizabeth, New Jersey, in 1901. Ordered with only two electric motors, it was found the cars were not up to the task. These trolleys were upgraded with four powerful Westinghouse motors in 1905. (Courtesy of Stanley F. Bowman Jr.)

North of the village of Ferndale, the trolley line left the roadside for a 1.5-mile run north to Kintnersville. This charming scene records the railroad-style trolley right-of-way skirting creek-side pastureland. Views like this inspired the authors of the *Wayside Scenes* trolley guidebook to describe the D&E as the "finest trolley ride in Pennsylvania. Where the meadow daisies grow. Where the rippled rivers flow." (Courtesy of James C. McHugh.)

Seen here in June 1908, the trolley north of Kintnersville ran along the west bank of the Delaware Canal. It was here in September 1906 that a crowd gathered to watch trolley car No. 6 attempt to tow a string of canal boats laden with 100 tons of anthracite coal. Although the trolley attained a speed of four miles per hour—twice that of a canal boat mule team—the experiment was not repeated. Trauger's Farm Market is situated just beyond the right edge of this view today. (Courtesy of the Solebury Township Historical Society.)

This rare photograph documents the 1921 improvement of Easton Road, with the D&E's trolley track running alongside. The uneven gravel road is being replaced with an 18-foot-wide cement concrete highway. The D&E was paid to use its work trolleys to haul construction materials for the contractor. The new all-weather road network, created by the state government, encouraged more automobile and motor truck traffic and hastened the end of the trolleys. (Courtesy of the Nockamixon Township Historical Commission.)

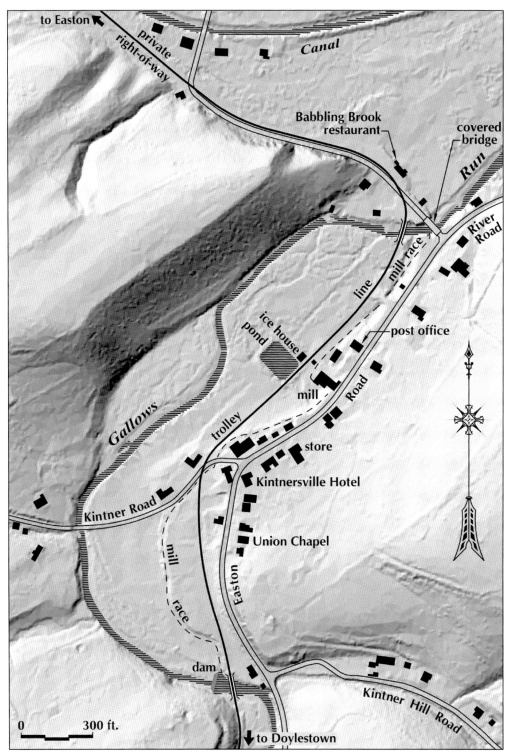

This map traces the alignment of the Doylestown & Easton trolley line through the village of Kintnersville in Nockamixon Township. (Drafted by the author.)

Rather than place its tracks along the road through the village of Kintnersville, the D&E purchased right-of-way behind backyards and past an ice pond. This view looks north and includes a trackside icehouse along with the conveyor ramp used to lift the heavy ice blocks. The old covered bridge that carried Easton Road across Gallows Run can be glimpsed beyond the icehouse. (Courtesy of James C. McHugh.)

The photographer is standing on Easton Road in Kintnersville and has aimed the camera west along Kintner Road, which bends sharply left. The short railing protects those crossing a small wooden bridge over a millrace. The house with the five second-story windows stands at 815 Kintner Road but is today screened by a dense stand of evergreen trees. The house in the foreground is 824 Kintner Road. With the rear pole raised against the wire, this trolley is headed south toward Doylestown. (Courtesy of Stanley F. Bowman Jr.)

Nestled along Easton Road between Kintnersville and Durham Furnace, visitors to the village of Monroe were offered comfortable canal-side accommodations at the Monroe Hotel. This photograph, taken from a vantage point on the high bluffs above town, shows trolley tracks and overhead wire brackets. Once a tranquil and scenic spot, today with Easton Road's 45-mile-per-hour speed limit, most people pass through what remains of the village before they know it. (Courtesy of the Solebury Township Historical Society.)

Three men and a dog stand before the Monroe Hotel. The name on the hotel sign is M.B. Shannon. This view looks south along Easton Road from the intersection with Lehnenburg Road. The September 6, 1896, issue of *Trips Awheel* warns bicyclists that they risk a $5 fine if caught riding on the canal towpath here (the equivalent of $150 dollars in 2020). The article also advises that the towpath is in no better condition than the parallel dirt road. (Courtesy of David F. Drinkhouse.)

This June 1908 view captures an Easton-bound trolley crossing the trolley bridge over Cook's Creek at Durham. The Durham Aqueduct carried Delaware Canal boats over the creek. Multifamily dwellings on the hillside beyond provided housing for Cooper, Hewitt & Company's Durham furnace workers and their families. (Courtesy of the Solebury Township Historical Society.)

The placid waters of the Delaware Canal reflect the image of southbound D&E trolley No. 6 in the summer of 1908. The view looks south along the canal towpath from a vantage point just south of Durham Furnace. The village of Monroe is a half mile south of this point. (Courtesy of the Solebury Township Historical Society.)

Passengers await the arrival of Easton-bound D&E trolley No. 11 at the corner of Delaware and Durham Roads in Riegelsville. Thanksgiving Day 1926 was the last day for these electric trolleys. Bean's Block on the right side of the street still stands but is two stories high rather than three. Tenants in 2020 include Guitar Parlor and Borderline Café. (Courtesy of Steven Cohen.)

Trolley track on the east edge of Canal Street passes the Riegelsville Central Hotel. The camera lens is pointed south along Canal Street from the intersection with Cedar Road; the Delaware Canal lies just out of view to the left. The building at 903 Durham Road is no longer a hotel but serves as a private residence today. (Courtesy of Stanley F. Bowman Jr.)

Bicyclists pedal south on Easton Road as northbound D&E trolley No. 3 awaits an oncoming trolley at switch No. 3 a mile north of Riegelsville. To the right of the trolley, a short bridge carrying the canal towpath over a Delaware Canal waste gate can be seen. The location is 100 yards above the Bucks County line in Williams Township, Northampton County. Today, Mueller's General Store and Kitchen occupies this spot. (Courtesy of David F. Drinkhouse.)

D&E's maintenance trolley known as the "Lily of the Valley" was built by partially dismantling old passenger car No. 103. Hopefully only used in fair weather, this car offered crewmen little protection from the elements. The man in the center is William J.B. Lines (1897–1984). The Delaware canal is just outside the right edge of the view. The house in the background still stands at 1239 Durham Road in Riegelsville. (Courtesy of David F. Drinkhouse.)

A fixture along Route 611 in Riegelsville for many years, this trolley never ran on the D&E line. The car body of former Northampton Transit car No. 110 was hauled to Riegelsville by truck years after the trolleys ceased running and placed on the northeast corner of Easton and Sycamore Roads. Seen here on May 30, 1950, Wilson's 611 Diner was swept off its foundations by Hurricane Diane's floodwaters on August 19, 1955. The 1903 Wason Manufacturing Company trolley was scrapped shortly thereafter. (Courtesy of James C. McHugh.)

A Doylestown & Easton Motor Coach Company bus rolls northbound on Main Street at Union Street in Doylestown on September 4, 1940. This block of Main Street was known as Germany Hill. The abandoned track to the Union Street trolley freight terminal can still be seen curving to the right. A subsidiary of PRT for many years, in 1944, the Doylestown to Easton bus route was purchased by Pennsylvania Greyhound Lines. (Courtesy of the collection of the Mercer Museum, Bucks County Historical Society.)

Six

QUAKERTOWN, PERKASIE, SELLERSVILLE
LIBERTY BELL HIGH-SPEED LINE

Lehigh Valley Transit Company's Liberty Bell line survived into the 1950s, outlasting other Bucks County trolleys by nearly two decades. Linking Allentown and Philadelphia, LVT's rapid and frequent electric freight and passenger cars served Quakertown, Perkasie, Sellersville, and local stops in between. This August 26, 1949, view finds passengers boarding red-and-cream high-speed trolley No. 1006 on North Main Street at Broad Street in Quakertown. (Photograph by Max H. Hubacher, courtesy of Railways to Yesterday Library.)

Electric trolley cars first ran on Ninth Street in Perkasie on January 19, 1900. Beginning in 1902, as through service between Allentown and Philadelphia commenced, passengers were carried on board these large, comfortable cars built by the St. Louis Car Company. Car No. 181 pauses at Perkasie Park. Not a public park, this evangelical Christian camp meeting's 60 Victorian cottages and vast outdoor auditorium date to 1882. In continuous operation since, Perkasie Park was listed in the National Register of Historic Places in 2016. (Author's collection.)

Trolley No. 173 is northbound near Derstines south of Sellersville around 1905. This roadside track, built by Inland Traction in 1900, was bypassed and removed in 1911. The delivery wagon at right is lettered Lit Brothers Philadelphia. A quarter-mile-long footpath led from this trolley stop to the evangelical Christian camp meeting known as Highland Park. Founded in 1893, its wood-frame tabernacle seats over 600. Highland Park was listed in the National Register of Historic Places in 2017. (Courtesy of the Sellersville Museum.)

A Philadelphia-bound LVT trolley pauses on Main Street at Walnut Street in Sellersville. This track had been built as Pennsylvania Broad Gauge, measuring 5 feet, 2.5 inches between rails. In May 1902, streets were dug up, and the rails pried loose from the wooden ties. Crews pushed the rails closer together by six inches, resulting in track of standard railroad gauge. Today, only a quarter of the old Sellersville Hotel building still stands, complete with corner turret, at 108 North Main Street. (Courtesy of Jerry Chiccarine.)

The crew of this Philadelphia-bound trolley have the street to themselves on a quiet day in Sellersville. The camera is pointed south along Main Street from a vantage point atop Washington House's six-story tower. Just beyond the trolley, the rails curve to the right as they approach the trolley bridge over East Branch Perkiomen Creek. The building with Central House painted on it is the same one labeled J.K. Renner at the top of this page, seen from the opposite side. (Courtesy of the Sellersville Museum.)

Officially chartered in November 1896, Quakertown Traction Company (QTC) was the first trolley line in the western part of Bucks County. This June 8, 1898, photograph captures the inaugural run from Broad Street in Quakertown to just below Richlandtown. QTC president C. Taylor Leland stands on the front step next to the windshield. (Courtesy of the Pennsylvania Trolley Museum.)

This pen-and-ink illustration depicts QTC's East Broad Street carbarn shortly after it opened in 1898. Once inside, the track fanned out into four tracks for car storage and maintenance. The castle-like stone building included coal-fired boilers and an electricity-generating plant. The building still stands in 2020. QNB Bank commissioned this work by James Mann for its Collector Calendars series. (Illustration by James Mann, courtesy of QNB Bank.)

This postcard view looks east on East Broad Street from the intersection with Belmont Avenue. The trolley barn is just outside the right edge of the photograph. Lehigh Valley Transit car No. 112 started out as Inland Traction car No. 1, one of two patented "Duplex cars" on the property. Informally referred to as barrel cars, the curved sides slid up into pockets above the ceiling similar to the way an old-fashioned roll-top desk worked. (Courtesy of Douglas E. Peters.)

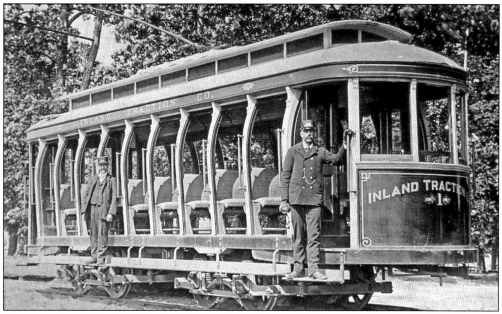

Costing a formidable $5,000 each when purchased new in 1900, two Duplex cars were painted red, white, and blue. Duplex car No. 1, seen here, is configured for warm weather, with the sides rolled up into the ceiling. The distance from the ground to the steps and running board could make climbing aboard early trolley cars a challenge. These two unique cars were assigned to the Quakertown to Richlandtown line until they were retired in 1915. (Courtesy of Andrew W. Maginnis.)

The intersection of Main and Broad Streets in Quakertown was a key location for trolleys from the first electric streetcars in 1898 to the end 53 years later. Known as Red Lion Junction, the historic Red Lion Inn has presided over this crossroads from long before the trolley era until today. This postcard view finds a Philadelphia-bound trolley leaving the scene to the left and one of the two Duplex cars headed to Richlandtown. (Author's collection.)

A Duplex car is stopped in front of Granville Straub's wholesale liquor store and bottling plant. The location is Hellertown Avenue opposite Erie Avenue. Prohibition would not be kind to this establishment, and a 1928 insurance atlas reveals no trace of it. Later, the Pilgrim Holiness Church was built on this spot, home today to the Quakertown Band. (Courtesy of the Railways to Yesterday Library.)

Both Duplex cars, one on the siding and one on the through track, occupy the 100 block of East Broad Street in Quakertown. The stone tower of the carbarn looms in the distance. The camera is pointed west from the intersection with Hellertown Avenue. Hissing, flickering carbon-arc lamps, such as the one hanging above the street, were more than adequate for lighting the intersection but would soon be replaced with incandescent lights. (Courtesy of Douglas E. Peters.)

Workers are closely scrutinized as they unload provisions for the Red Lion Inn in Quakertown. Before motor trucks were reliable, and before roads were paved to run them on, trolley freight was relied upon by all manner of businesses along the line. The photographer looks east on Broad Street toward the trolley junction at Main Street. The Red Lion Inn is outside the right edge of the image. (Courtesy of the Steve Moyer collection, Lansdale Historical Society.)

Because Reading Railroad would not allow trolley tracks to cross the railroad at grade, Quakertown Traction Company built this bridge over the railroad in 1898. Its location is detailed on the map below. A series of short spans supported by wooden timbers ramped up to the spindly steel truss that spanned the railroad. The bridge served its purpose until the last trolley rumbled across on June 15, 1929. (Courtesy of the Pennsylvania Trolley Museum.)

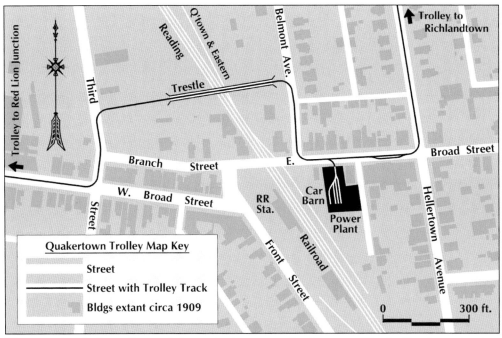

This map details the trolley track layout in downtown Quakertown. (Drafted by the author.)

106

The 3.5-mile trolley line from Quakertown's Red Lion Junction to Richlandtown opened in 1898. After trolley track was laid across the Quakertown & Eastern Railroad crossing a half mile south of Richlandtown in 1907, a single trolley was enough to provide hourly service. This May 31, 1929, photograph was taken two weeks before gasoline-burning buses took over. The address of the house at left is 26 North Main Street, Richlandtown. (Courtesy of Douglas E. Peters)

The Richlandtown line suffered a minor mishap around 1905. Because the Quakertown & Eastern Railroad would not allow trolleys to cross at grade, LVT operated the line in two segments. This simple wood-frame barn, plastered with wheat-paste advertisements, housed the trolley isolated north of the crossing. Here, car No. 52 has burst through the rear wall of the barn. Only after the Q&E suspended service in 1907 was LVT permitted to install its grade crossing and provide an uninterrupted ride. (Courtesy of Douglas E. Peters.)

An LVT interurban trolley passes through the village of Zion Hill in Springfield Township. Trolleys used these rails between 1902 and 1925. After 1925, trolleys used the railroad-style Rosedale cutoff through the fields a quarter mile to the west (beyond the left edge of this view). The house at left, its curved wood brackets still supporting the porch roof, stands at 2996 Old Bethlehem Pike. Although located four miles north of town, this residence is today served by the Quakertown Post Office. (Courtesy of Steven Cohen.)

Southbound LVT trolley No. 154 is fast approaching the Bucks County line south of Coopersburg in 1924. This north-facing photograph was taken by Frederick E. Barber, an electrical engineer with the LVT company. A devoted trolley enthusiast, Railways to Yesterday's LVT archives in Allentown were named in Barber's honor. This roadside trackage would be removed after the Rosedale cutoff opened the following year. (Courtesy of the Railways to Yesterday Library.)

The small hamlet of Rocky Ridge along Old Bethlehem Pike between Quakertown and Perkasie was served by LVT trolleys for over 50 years until 1951, when the electric interurban service was abandoned. The Rocky Ridge Hotel served as an important roadside hostelry since 1812. Prior to the North Penn Railroad's completion in 1857, droves of horse-drawn vehicles of all kinds trod Old Bethlehem Pike right outside the tavern's doors. Overnight accommodations included a large stable across the road. When a new state highway diverted most automobile traffic off this road, LVT's freight and passenger trolleys still stopped here. The venerable building is today an apartment house. The above postcard view looks south; the one below faces north at the same location. Even with a trolley bearing down on him, the bicyclist (above) is safe riding in the center of the road, with the trolley track off to one side. Several families have turned out (below) to stand for the camera with Philadelphia-bound LVT car No. 150. (Both, courtesy of Steven Cohen.)

On December 12, 1912, the Lehigh Valley Transit Company inaugurated high-speed service between Allentown and Philadelphia over an alignment that included center-of-street rails, side-of-the-road tracks, and railroad-style bypasses. Implemented between 1910 and 1913, the new segments of right-of-way and new freight and passenger cars represented a $5 million investment. LVT's claim to having the finest electric trains in the world was no idle boast. Built by high-end railcar builder Jewett Car Company, the twelve 800 series cars weighed in at 40 tons apiece and were capable of mile-a-minute speed—no mean feat in 1912. A September 7, 1936, photograph captures car No. 800 northbound (above) at Quakertown station along with a front-engine bus, owned by Warren B. Levy, bound for downtown Quakertown and Richlandtown. With passenger comfort a priority, the interurban trolleys were equipped with restrooms (left). (Above, courtesy of James C. McHugh; left, courtesy of Andrew W. Maginnis.)

This late 1911 view looking northeast on Ninth Street in Perkasie captures both the old and the new trolley alignments. The rails in the center of the street have been in use since 1900. Once trolley traffic is diverted to the new high-speed bypass over the plate girder bridge, the track in the street will be torn out. The entrance to Perkasie Park is just beyond the left edge of the frame. (Courtesy of Andrew W. Maginnis.)

Car No. 812 stops on Walnut Street at Penn Street in Perkasie on February 22, 1947. Resembling the 800 series Jewett interurbans, car No. 812 was built by LVT's in-house shop forces in 1914. Constructed on the frame of wrecked car No. 159, car No. 999 was a private car replete with a clubroom, liquor cabinet, cigar humidor, dining room with seating for 18, and a kitchen. Its most notable passenger was former US president William H. Taft. In 1921, it was renumbered, and its splendid interior remodeled for regular passenger service. (Photograph by Charles A. Brown.)

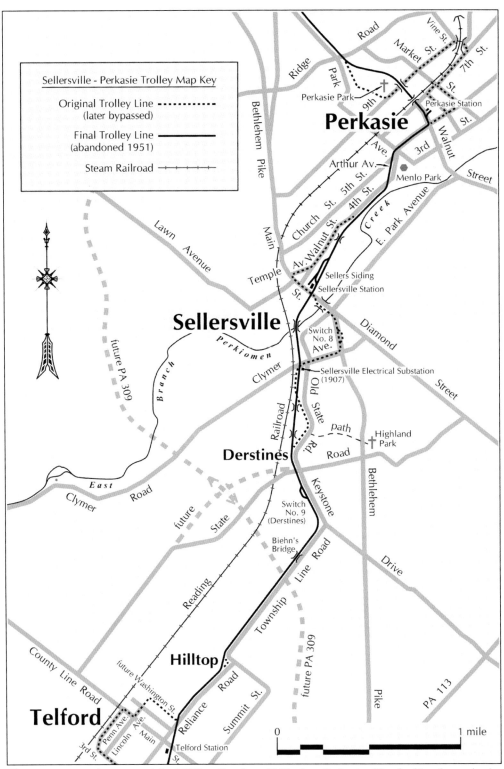

This map traces the route of the LVT trolley from Telford to Perkasie. (Drafted by the author).

Freight is being loaded onto northbound LVT freight motor C2 at Sellersville Station in 1916. In later years, a stub-end siding would be constructed behind the station so that the loading and unloading of freight cars could be accomplished without blocking passenger trolleys. Heavy steel brackets jutting out from the front, along with the lower portion of the center window blocked off, serve as reminders that this workhorse also served as a snowplow during winter months. (Courtesy of Andrew W. Maginnis.)

After it was apparent that the promised trolley line between Perkasie and Doylestown would not be built, LVT motorman Charles Sprague saw an opportunity. Sprague owned the Perkasie-Doylestown Auto Bus Line, running five round trips each day. This photograph features Sprague's new 15-passenger REO Speed Wagon in front of 124 North Sixth Street in Perkasie. At 65¢, the fare between the towns was rather high ($10 in 2020 dollars). By the late 1920s, the line was losing money. Bus service ended in 1930. (Courtesy of Douglas E. Peters.)

Located astride the transition zone between the Atlantic coastal plane and the Piedmont, Bucks County's winter weather runs the gamut from all-day rains to all-out blizzards. Midway between those poles lies one of the most destructive of winter events, the freezing rain storm. When rain falls onto ground or onto objects that are below freezing, the liquid freezes on contact, forming a glaze that can weigh down tree limbs and snap power lines. These photographs reveal the dramatic effects of ice storms in the early and later years of the trolley line. With the photographer credited as simply "Weider" (above), the entire overhead power system near Quakertown needed rebuilding after a December 29, 1915, storm. A January 1, 1948, storm (below) glazed the overhead wires, leaving southbound car No. 1005 stranded for three days behind the backyard of a house on Walnut Street in Sellersville. (Above, courtesy of the Railways to Yesterday Library; below, courtesy of the Sellersville Museum.)

A southbound 700 series car is about to pass beneath Trolley Bridge Road on the Rosedale cutoff in Springfield Township. This is near the village of Zion Hill, which is seen in the photograph at the top of page 108. In 1925, LVT spent $450,000 to build five miles of railroad-style right-of-way, bypassing the ever-increasing motor vehicle traffic on five miles of roads, notably Main Street in Coopersburg. In other places, track remained on the side of the road through to the end in 1951. (Courtesy of the Pennsylvania Trolley Museum.)

Working as a snowplow, southbound LVT freight motor C7 is on Walnut Street at Sixth Street in Perkasie. This freight car and two others were ordered from Jewett at the same time as the second batch of palatial 800 series cars in 1913. The green Breyers Ice Cream sign on the right was a common sight outside Southeastern Pennsylvania grocery stores for decades. The driver of the automobile in the foreground has wisely applied chains to the rear wheels. (Photograph by Lester K. Wismer.)

Refurbished trolleys burst onto the scene in early 1939. LVT purchased 13 used high-speed railcars from the Cincinnati & Lake Erie Railroad and reconditioned them to serve as Liberty Bell Limiteds. The streamlined aluminum-bodied trolleys were capable of speeds well in excess of 80 miles per hour. New York public relations firm Hill & Knowlton was hired to promote the enhanced service. (Courtesy of the John R. Neiveen collection, Andrew W. Maginnis.)

This view documents high-speed car No. 1004's interior. The round window penetrates the bulkhead dividing the straight seating from the rear observation compartment. A compact restroom is at right. The interior of each "ten hundred" series car was designed individually, with fabrics in a variety of color combinations and with leather or mohair seat covers. A finishing touch was the cloth headrest cover with an embroidered Liberty Bell logo. (Courtesy of the Howard P. Sell collection, Railways to Yesterday Library.)

These passengers' wait is over as southbound LVT car No. 1020 pulls into Sellersville Station on May 3, 1941. Painted cream with bright-red trim by LVT, these trolleys were designed in 1930 to race hundreds of miles across Ohio, connecting Cincinnati and Toledo. When the Cincinnati & Lake Erie Railroad ended passenger service and 20 of these cars were put up for sale in 1938, the LVT purchased 13, overhauling them at its shops in Allentown. (Photograph by L.S. Dietrich, courtesy of the Railways to Yesterday Library.)

LVT's 1939 equipment upgrade included refurbished trolleys for local service. Six ex-Steubenville, Ohio, cars capable of 60-mile-per-hour speed were rebuilt with modernized front ends. Built in 1926, the cars bore no fleet numbers in Ohio, being named instead for Ohio cities. This car was the *Toronto*. Bright-red northbound car No. 434 is starting to cross from the east side of Old Bethlehem Pike to the west on August 24, 1943. Today, the Quakertown Main Street Skatepark is on the right side, across the street. (Courtesy of James C. McHugh.)

These two photographs capture LVT ten hundred series trolleys passing the historic Rich Hill store on Old Bethlehem Pike in Richland Township. The above view shows car No. 1007 northbound on Memorial Day, May 30, 1947. The photograph below shows car No. 1021 southbound on a winter day in 1950. Originally known as Bunker Hill, this early 1800s building once housed a tavern operated by Anthony Amey. After the eventual loss of its license, the building served for many years as a post office and general store. During the time of the trolley, tickets were sold, and a waiting room was made available for passengers. In later years, various proprietors at different times operated the grocery store, soda fountain, and lunch counter. The store closed in the 1960s. The building was torn down in 2018. (Above, courtesy of the Pennsylvania Trolley Museum; below, photograph by David H. Cope.)

When one of the ten hundred series cars was consumed by fire in December 1940, a replacement was sought. Indiana Railroad club car No. 55 fit the bill. Built in 1931 by American Car & Foundry, it was similar in capability and appearance to the ex-C&LE cars. Renumbered 1030, it entered LVT service in October 1941. Its armchairs were replaced by regular seating in 1949. Southbound No. 1030 is on Walnut Street in Perkasie in August 1950. Car No. 1030 is preserved at Seashore Trolley Museum in Maine. (Courtesy of James C. McHugh.)

Before it officially entered service, car No. 1030 was chartered for an excursion including round trips to Easton and to Norristown. This photograph finds members and guests of the National Railway Historical Society Lehigh Valley Chapter enjoying No. 1030's luxurious interior on September 28, 1941. The man at right is none other than John Gibb Smith. Selections from the vast collection of trolley photographs that Smith donated to the Free Library of Philadelphia in 1946 are featured in chapter two. (Courtesy of James C. McHugh.)

Only a single lane has been cleared of snow for motor vehicle traffic on Old Bethlehem Pike a quarter mile south of Tollgate Road in Richland Township. The camera is facing north on March 9, 1947. The arrow-straight line of poles receding into the distance gives a sense of the speed these trolleys could attain along this stretch of road. In 2020, the house still stands at 1175 Old Bethlehem Pike, Quakertown. (Courtesy of the Pennsylvania Trolley Museum.)

With the sun shining brightly the day after a heavy snowfall, an intrepid photographer has climbed up onto the Reading Railroad Bethlehem Branch to photograph a southbound ten hundred series car entering Perkasie. The trolley has just crossed the bridge over Ninth Street and is about to enter the tunnel bored through the railroad embankment. Despite the danger, many pedestrians used the narrow trolley tunnel as a shortcut. (Courtesy of the Pennsylvania Trolley Museum.)

Thin ice covers East Branch Perkiomen Creek adjacent to Sellersville Station, reflecting a northbound LVT Limited. This ten hundred series interurban car has just passed the spring switch at the south end of Sellersville siding. Built in 1910, this section of trolley right-of-way today serves as a paved bike path. Part of the Sellersville–Perkasie–East Rockhill Township Bicycle/Walking Path System, the trails provide car-free access to parks, schools, and other points of interest in three municipalities. (Courtesy of Andrew W. Maginnis.)

Wood Siding was located at the grade crossing where the LVT Philadelphia Division crossed Old Bethlehem Pike two miles north of Quakertown. Because the trolley line crossed the highway at an oblique angle, oncoming trolleys could be hidden from motorists' view. When loud train whistles, flashing warning lights, and clanging bells were ignored, grade-crossing collisions ensued. The worst, on July 2, 1938, claimed six lives. The house at right still stands at 2550 Old Bethlehem Pike, Quakertown. (Courtesy of James C. McHugh.)

Perhaps referring to the ethnicity of members of the work crew, the words IRISH LOCAL have been lettered in chalk on the side of maintenance car No. 502. The location is the first 100 feet of the Richlandtown Branch, just east of Red Lion Junction in Quakertown. The address of the building behind the trolley is 1239 West Broad Street. (Courtesy of the Railways to Yesterday Library.)

Built to maintain and repair overhead trolley wire, LVT line car R1 occupies the through track at Wood Siding, two miles north of Quakertown. Based at Fairview carbarn in Allentown, R1 was a 1912 product of the Russell Car and Snow-Plow Company of Ridgway, Pennsylvania. Russell products were known for their solid construction and rugged dependability. Old Bethlehem Pike is immediately outside the right frame of the photograph. (Courtesy of Douglas E. Peters.)

This February 15, 1951, view captures a southbound trolley freight train consisting of cars C19, C15, and C16 at Ridge Siding along Old Bethlehem Pike a mile and a half north of Perkasie. The 20-foot-wide strip of right-of-way containing the passing siding is today owned by the Pennsylvania Power & Light Company. The house at right is 1917 Old Bethlehem Pike. (Courtesy of James C. McHugh.)

Lester K. Wismer of Souderton made it his mission to document the final years of the Liberty Bell line. Wismer's excellent eye for composition resulted in views such as this 1946 photograph of a northbound ten hundred series car rushing past Sellersville Substation at Clymer Avenue. Built in 1908, massive rotary converters housed here changed high-voltage alternating current to the 600-volt direct current that energized the trolley wire. The wood sign affixed to the pole at left identifies this as stop No. 75. (Photograph by Lester K. Wismer, courtesy of the Railways to Yesterday Library.)

The driver and four passengers of this automobile escaped with their lives when motorist Frederick Freer of West Philadelphia stalled his auto on the LVT tracks in Sellersville on Sunday, June 12, 1949. Bound for Perkasie's Menlo Park, Freer turned onto an earth-surface lane off Walnut Street, thinking that it led to parking for Menlo Park up the road. Grade-crossing collisions were an all too frequent occurrence along the Liberty Bell line. (Photograph by John H. Brinckmann Jr., courtesy of Richard S. Short.)

At 6:00 p.m. on Thursday, September 6, 1951, LVT suddenly announced that would be the final day of electric trolley service on its Philadelphia division. The next morning, passengers would board slow diesel buses running on nearby roads, a vastly inferior service that would cease within five years. Here, the last Liberty Bell trolley is about to depart Eight and Hamilton Streets in Allentown at 11:06 p.m. On hand are, from left to right, Paul Moyer, superintendent; Fred Enters Jr., operator; and Guy Kutzler, inspector. (Courtesy of James C. McHugh.)

Seven

BUCKINGHAM VALLEY TROLLEY ASSOCIATION

TROLLEY VALHALLA

Between 1975 and 1980, electric trolley cars mounted a brief comeback in Bucks County. Trolley Valhalla, an antique trolley operation in Jobstown, New Jersey, found itself in need of a home. New Hope & Ivyland (NH&I) Railroad, operator of steam-hauled tourist trains on the former Reading Railroad New Hope Branch, agreed to allow overhead trolley wire to be strung over a portion of the railroad. Dedicated volunteers reorganized as the Buckingham Valley Trolley Association (BVTA), and trolley rides were offered to the public. Passengers could disembark from the NH&I steam train during its layover at Buckingham Station near Durham Road at Upper Mountain Road and ride a trolley one mile south on the railroad to Creek Road in Buckingham Township and return. (Courtesy of Joel Salomon.)

Northbound BVTA car No. 26 crosses a driveway at 1732 Creek Road in Buckingham Township. Car No. 26 was one of a fleet of 130 "Hog Island" trolleys ordered by the federal government in 1918 to get Philadelphia workers to wartime shipyards. Originally numbered 4024, this and two others were purchased by Philadelphia Suburban Transportation during World War II. In 1964, car No. 26 was saved from the scrapper's torch by members of the Metropolitan Philadelphia Railway Association. BVTA moved its trolleys to Delaware Avenue along Philadelphia's waterfront in 1982, only ceasing operations there when a street-widening project forced them off. (Courtesy of Joel Salomon.)

New Hope & Ivyland Railroad president James C. McHugh delivers opening remarks during inaugural ceremonies of the BVTA trolley operation on Sunday, June 1, 1975. McHugh, known to his friends as Jimmy, was instrumental in making the BVTA happen. He was co-owner of McHugh Brothers Heavy Hauling and served as vice chair of the Southeastern Pennsylvania Transportation Authority (SEPTA) board of directors. McHugh generously made available his wonderful collection of Bucks County trolley memorabilia, photographs, and postcards, many of which are featured in the pages of this book. He passed away in November 2019 as this book was being prepared, and is missed by his family and friends. (Courtesy of Joel Salomon.)

BIBLIOGRAPHY

Coates, Wes. *Electric Trains to Reading Terminal.* Flanders, NJ: Railroad Avenue Enterprises Inc., 1990.

Cox, Harold E. *Utility Cars of Philadelphia 1892–1971.* Forty Fort, PA: Harold E. Cox, 1971.

Davis, William W.H. *History of Bucks County Pennsylvania from the Discovery of the Delaware to the Present Time.* New York, NY: Lewis Publishing Company, 1905.

DeGraw, Ronald. *The Red Arrow.* Haverford, PA: Haverford Press, 1972.

Drinkhouse, David F. *Doylestown and Easton Street Railway, the Road of Wild Roses.* Easton, PA: self-published, 2013.

Foesig, Harry, et al. *Trolleys of Bucks County Pennsylvania.* Forty Fort, PA: Harold E. Cox, 1985.

Gummere, Barker. *Street Railways of Trenton.* Forty Fort, PA: Harold E. Cox, 1986.

Gummere, Barker, and Gary Kleinedler. *Trenton-Princeton Traction Company: Pennsylvania and New Jersey Railway.* Wheaton, IL: Traction Orange Company, 1966.

Hilton, George W., and John F. Due. *The Electric Interurban Railways in America.* Stanford, CA: Stanford University Press, 1960.

Kulp, Randolph L., ed. *History of Lehigh Valley Transit Company.* Allentown, PA: Lehigh Valley Chapter, National Railway Historical Society, 1966.

————. *Short Trolley Routes in the Lehigh River Valley.* Allentown, PA: Lehigh Valley Chapter, National Railway Historical Society, 1967.

Leary, Jane Kiefer. *Trolley Memories of a Raubsville Resident.* Easton, PA: Northampton County Historical & Genealogical Society, 2013.

McKelvey, William J. Jr. *Lehigh Valley Transit Company's Liberty Bell Route.* Berkeley Heights, NJ: Canal Captain's Press, 1989.

Messer, David W., and Charles S. Roberts. *Triumph V, Philadelphia to New York, 1830–2002.* Baltimore, MD: Barnard, Roberts and Company, 2002.

Ruddell, Ron. *Riding the Bell: Lehigh Valley Transit's Liberty Bell Route.* Chicago, IL: Central Electric Railfans' Association, 2015.

DISCOVER THOUSANDS OF LOCAL HISTORY BOOKS
FEATURING MILLIONS OF VINTAGE IMAGES

Arcadia Publishing, the leading local history publisher in the United States, is committed to making history accessible and meaningful through publishing books that celebrate and preserve the heritage of America's people and places.

Find more books like this at
www.arcadiapublishing.com

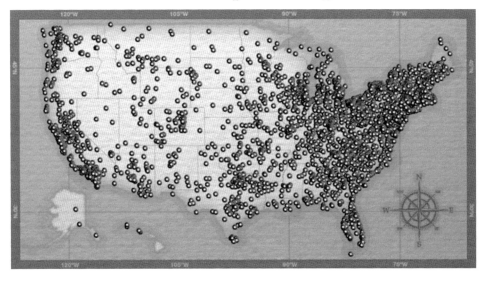

Search for your hometown history, your old stomping grounds, and even your favorite sports team.

Consistent with our mission to preserve history on a local level, this book was printed in South Carolina on American-made paper and manufactured entirely in the United States. Products carrying the accredited Forest Stewardship Council (FSC) label are printed on 100 percent FSC-certified paper.

MADE IN THE

USA